£6.00

THE ILLUSTRATED ENCYCLOPEDIA OF

FLOWERING
PLANTS

THE ILLUSTRATED ENCYCLOPEDIA OF
FLOWERING PLANTS

by Bohdan Křísa
edited by Pamela Bristow

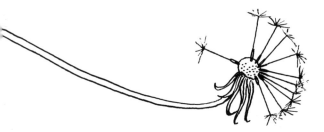

SELECT
EDITIONS

Picture Acknowledgements
(Figures refer to numbers of illustrations)

Bílý, Svatopluk: 199
Blahout, Milič: p. 9
Chroust Miloslav: p. 24
Čihař, Jiří: 159, 161—163, 167, 168, 171, 172, 175, 176, 178, 180, 182—185, 187, 190—193, 195, 198, 199, 201, 202, 205, 210
Čihař, Martin: frontispiece, 160, 164, 177, 179, 181, 188, 189, 194, 203, 204
Feyfar, Zdenko: 166, 173, 179, 187
Gregor, Karel: 8, p. 23, 133, 153, 197, 206, 224, 231, 236, 299, 304, 325, 369
Jaroš, Miroslav: 3, 4, 9, 11, 12, 16, 17, 21, 22, 26, 27, 30, 35, 36, 119, 120, 148, 149, 157, 158, 165, 169, 174, 208, 209, 212, 213, 216, 217, 221—223, 226, 230, 232, 233, 241, 242, 245—247, 250—252, 255, 256, 259—261, 264—266, 269—271, 274—276, 279—281, 289, 290, 294, 298, 311—313, 317, 324, 329, 330, 334, 335, 338—340, 343, 344, 349, 353, 354, 363, 364, 368, 370, 373
Krýsl, Jan: 1, 5—7, 10, 13—15, 18—20, 23—25, 28, 29, 32—34, 88, 91, 92, 94, 99, 102, 117, 127, 135, 136, 139, 140, 145, 147, 150, 151, 207, 211, 214, 218, 219, 225, 228, 229, 234, 235, 238—240, 243, 244, 248, 249, 253, 254, 257, 258, 262, 263, 268, 273, 278, 291, 292, 295, 297, 303, 305—308, 314, 318, 319, 322, 331—333, 336, 341, 342, 347, 348, 352, 356, 357, 361, 362, 367, 371, 372, p. 18
Lewis Smith, R. I., British Antarctic Survey: p. 17
Lukavský, Jaromír: 130, 137, 138, 141, 14.?, 144, 152, 154—156
Měsíček, Josef: 186
Novák, F. A.: 170, 196, 200, 363, pp. 12, 13, 14, 15
Pavlík, Přemysl: 2, 31, 83, 84, 215, 272, ?77
Sýkora, Tomáš: 237
Štursa, Jan: 227
Šubík, Rudolf: p. 16, 37—82, 85—87, 89, 90, 93, 95—98, 100, 101, 103—116, 118, 121—126, 128, 129, 131, 132, 134, 143, 146, 220, 267, 282—288, 293, 296, 300—302, 309, 310, 315, 316, 320, 321, 323, 326—328, 337, 345, 346, 350, 351, 355, 358—360, 365, 366
Waltham, A. C.: p. 25

Text by Bohdan Křísa
Translated by Olga Kuthanová
Graphic design by František Prokeš

This edition published 1992 by
The Promotional Reprint Co Ltd,
Chelsea Chambers, 262 A Fulham Road,
London SW10 9EL

ISBN 1 85648 067 4
Printed in Czechoslovakia by SPEKTRUM BRNO
3/11/05/51-02

CONTENTS

Alpine Aster *(Aster alpinus)* (description on page 201).

FOREWORD

The purpose of this book is to acquaint
the reader with certain interesting species of flowering plants and to relate
their morphological features to their
environments and to their geographic
distributions. Some 400 species, subspecies and hybrids make up the 11 chapters of this book, assembled to stress
first and foremost the biological pecu-
liarities of the individual plants.

PLANT ECOLOGY

Every plant is part of a biome or ecosystem (a complex of plant and animal communities and their environment) with ecological relationships to atmosphere, soil and water and to other plants and animals. Every region has several types of ecosystems, depending upon its geographic location and altitude above sea level. These differ in the composition of plant and animal species and in the environmental factors — climate, rock substrates, soil, man's activities, etc. The earth's total biosphere is divided into zones determined by the existing climate; these differ in the amount of rainfall, minimum and maximum temperature, annual seasons, and length of day and night. This, in turn, determines the type of vegetation — coniferous forests in the temperate zone, tundra communities in the arctic zone, and tropical rain forests in the equatorial zone.

Plant communities often have very specific ecological requirements, for instance aquatic and shoreline communities require water. Terrestrial and aquatic 'worlds' may not always appear to be distinctly separate, however the plants and animals of these two 'worlds' differ markedly. From the viewpoint of their life functions the barriers between the two are insurmountable. There are many similar isolating barriers in nature and so a great diversity of organisms has evolved, each one uniquely adapted to its own environment. In many communities a phenomenon occurs called succession. Succession is accompanied by a gradual change of plant species, the successive displacement of one kind by another, followed by changes in the soil. Such a change is seen in the slow silting up of a pond with the subsequent change from an aquatic flora, through a shoreline one to a marsh and then to a totally terrestrial plant community. Seasonal changes also occur that affect the nature and appearance of the vegetation.

Soil and climate are factors that are essential too and play a decisive role in the development of plant communities. Climatic factors include water, temperature and light while soils differ chiefly in the chemical and physical properties of their minerals. Let us take a look at the importance and function of some of these factors.

Water is essential to the growth of all plants and the amount of water in the plant tissues changes not only according to the water conditions of the given environment but also according to the ability of the plants to absorb water and limit evaporation. Somewhat unusual in this respect are the xerophilous (drought-loving) plants, which are well able to withstand dry conditions. A special group are the succulents, for instance cacti and spurges, whose fleshy leaves and stems with large stores of water enable the plants to withstand both lack of water as well as high temperatures.

Heat is an equally important factor, for plants are capable of growth only within certain atmospheric and soil temperature limits. These limits are different for each individual species. The diversity in the earth's plant cover from the equator to the poles is caused mainly by the differences in temperature of the air and soil. High mountain and northern plants include many species that tolerate extremely low winter temperatures, often around minus 50°C. On the other hand the maximum temperatures at which life processes still function are as high as 50° to 55° in succulents and only from 30° to 40°C in other land plants. There is no doubt that the maximum temperatures tolerated by plants of temperate regions differ from those tolerated by plants growing in the tropics. According to their relationship to heat plants are described either as warmth-loving (thermophilic) or cold-loving (psychrophilic). In temperate regions the latter group also includes spring species whose optimum period of growth is during the period of relatively low nighttime and daytime temperatures. Such spring plants may be rightfully termed cold-loving.

Light is another important factor affecting the growth of all plants either directly or indirectly. Autotrophic plants, that is green plants containing chlorophyll, need light in the form of radiant energy (sunlight) to produce organic matter. Parasitic and saprophytic plants which lack green colouring matter (chlorophyll) are dependent on light indirectly, through the agency of the green plants on which their growth depends.

8

An alpine ecosystem.

The presence of oxygen and other gases is also essential to plants, although these factors are far more constant in a terrestrial environment than are light, heat or water. Oxygen is required for breathing, for the energy needed to obtain water and nourishment, for their transport throughout the plant body, for storing reserve food, and last but not least for growth and movement. Carbon dioxide (CO_2) is of special importance, for it is essential to the process of photosynthesis, along with water, light and chlorophyll.

In some of the descriptions of the plants in this book special note is taken of the parent rock on which they grow. Basic rocks weather and change into soil with ample amounts of lime and magnesium and form a substrate which supports a wealth of widely diverse plants. Limestones, dolomites and marls form extraordinarily good substrates for plant communities and so calcicolous (lime-demanding) plants are far greater in number and in diversity of species than are silicicolous plants, those that thrive in soil formed by the weathering of acidic (silicic) rocks.

9

THE DISTRIBUTION OF PLANTS

The present distribution of plant communities and plant species is the result of the long term changes that have taken place during the history of life on Earth. This distribution is not final. Every region has natural barriers such as rivers, deserts, mountains or seas, which may sometimes be insurmountable and prevent the spread of plants. Separate communities then develop on each side of the barrier. The extent, location and area of distribution of various plant species may differ widely. Plants do not usually form a continuous cover throughout an area but are scattered according to the configuration of the landscape and to their specific ecological requirements. The following chapters will introduce us to plants that are cosmopolitan, that is they have a worldwide distribution, as well as to species that are restricted to a particular region or even to a single locality. The distribution of most plant species lies somewhere between these two extremes. The section on aquatic and shoreline plants, for instance, includes species that have cosmopolitan distributions because of the ecological similarity of inland bodies of water throughout the world. On the other hand there are a great many plants whose beauty we can admire only in a few places (sometimes only in a single place) on Earth.

The zonality of the Earth is determined by the climate prevailing at various distances from the equator and the poles. Some of these zones are referred to in the text for the distribution of many species is limited by these zones (belts). In the northern hemisphere the zones are as follows from the equator northward: tropical zone, subtropical zone, meridional zone (at the

The world's principal vegetational zones and floristic regions.

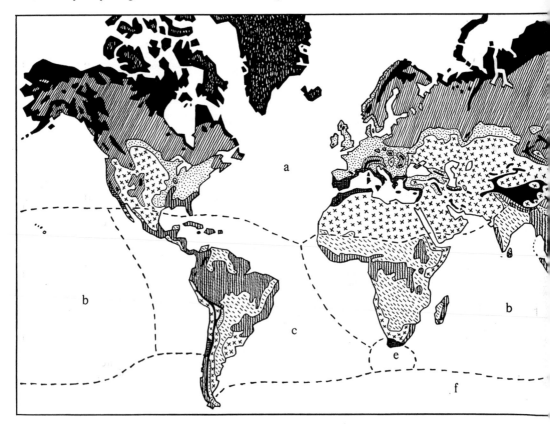

same latitude as the Mediterranean), temperate zone, boreal zone, and arctic zone. In the southern hemisphere the divisions are similar but less pronounced.

Climatic-vegetational belts are not determined solely by latitude, of course. They are also greatly affected by the closeness of oceans and the configuration of mountain massifs, factors which alter the latitude of the zones in Europe when compared to North America.

FLORISTIC REGIONS OF THE WORLD

Every region is distinguished by the presence of a certain number of plant species, whose occurrence and distribution is determined by horizontal zones and altitudinal belts. The plant life characteristic of a territory is termed the flora of that region. The flora of various continents and countries differs markedly and the world can be divided according to the presence of certain plant species, genera or families into several floristic regions, which may be further divided into provinces and even smaller regional units. Because the species depicted in this book represent the flora of all continents — South America, Australia, Africa, Asia, Europe and North America — we will take note only of the large floristic regions. In the northern hemisphere there is one floristic region outside the tropics, the tropics have two and the southern hemisphere has three floristic regions outside the tropics. The explanation often given for this is that the southern part of the original landmass split much earlier than the northern part.

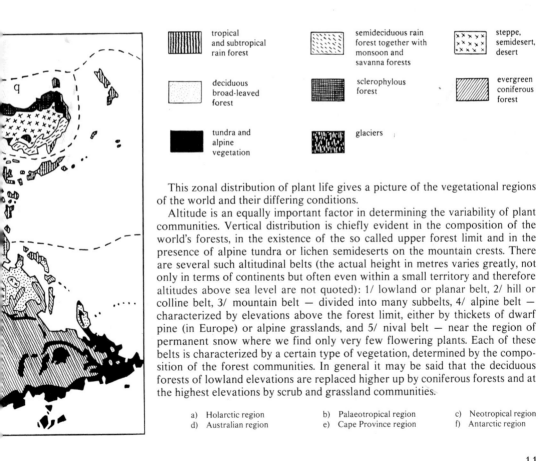

tropical and subtropical rain forest	semideciduous rain forest together with monsoon and savanna forests	steppe, semidesert, desert
deciduous broad-leaved forest	sclerophylous forest	evergreen coniferous forest
tundra and alpine vegetation	glaciers	

This zonal distribution of plant life gives a picture of the vegetational regions of the world and their differing conditions.

Altitude is an equally important factor in determining the variability of plant communities. Vertical distribution is chiefly evident in the composition of the world's forests, in the existence of the so called upper forest limit and in the presence of alpine tundra or lichen semideserts on the mountain crests. There are several such altitudinal belts (the actual height in metres varies greatly, not only in terms of continents but often even within a small territory and therefore altitudes above sea level are not quoted): 1/ lowland or planar belt, 2/ hill or colline belt, 3/ mountain belt — divided into many subbelts, 4/ alpine belt — characterized by elevations above the forest limit, either by thickets of dwarf pine (in Europe) or alpine grasslands, and 5/ nival belt — near the region of permanent snow where we find only very few flowering plants. Each of these belts is characterized by a certain type of vegetation, determined by the composition of the forest communities. In general it may be said that the deciduous forests of lowland elevations are replaced higher up by coniferous forests and at the highest elevations by scrub and grassland communities.

a) Holarctic region   b) Palaeotropical region   c) Neotropical region
d) Australian region   e) Cape Province region   f) Antarctic region

11

The Holarctic region includes the whole northern hemisphere excepting the tropical regions and embraces all of North America, Europe, northern Asia and north Africa. On the American continent its influence extends along the mountain ranges deep into northern Mexico. The plant life is relatively stable though within such a vast territory there are naturally differences in the representation of genera and families, influenced particularly by the glacial periods and an unequal postglacial evolution.

Spring Anemone *(Pulsatilla vernalis)* — a plant of montane and submontane meadows and rocky slopes in the Holarctic region.

The Palaeotropical region includes all the tropical regions of the Old World, that is most of Africa including Madagascar, south and southeast Asia including the Indo-Malayan Archipelago and the Pacific islands excepting the Galapagos and other smaller islands off the coast of South America. It is noteworthy for the presence of certain families that are absent in other parts of the world such as the succulent spurge family (Euphorbiaceae), many epiphytic orchids and certain plants of the lily family (the genus *Aloë*).

Various species of the genus *Aloë* are typical representatives of the flora of semiarid African regions.

The Neotropical region embraces the tropics of the New World, that is Central America and practically all of South America, including the Caribbean islands and the Galapagos Islands off the coast of Ecuador. The flora of this territory has a very distinctive character and numbers many thousands of peculiar species (orchids, bromeliads, cacti) distributed either in the tropical regions of Brazil or the high-mountain altiplanos of the South American Andes. It abounds in diversity of species, fascinating shapes and bewitching colours.

The Australian region is unique in that it embraces only a small continent (Australia) which contains numerous endemic species and genera. The composition of the flora of the southwestern part of the continent somewhat resembles that of South Africa.

Aechmea fasciata is one of the numerous bromeliads which contribute to the brightness of the South American rain forest.

Southwestern Australia is characterized by plants of the family Proteaceae; this one is *Grevillea jumperina.*

The semideserts of the Cape Province region abound in succulents of the family Mesembryanthemaceae. Some species show a remarkable resemblance to pebbles and only for a short time show their vividly coloured flowers.

The Cape Province region is the smallest of all in terms of area for it includes only the southern tip of Africa and because it is separated from the rest of Africa by a barrier of deserts and savannas has a specific flora of its own with a great many endemic plants, some of which are also found in Australia. One example of the South African flora is the large mesembryanthemum (Mesembryanthemaceae) family of fleshy-leaved plants whose remarkable mimicry decorates the semideserts of this part of the continent.

Tufts of Antarctic Pearlwort *Colobanthus quitensis,* one of only two species of flowering plants on the Antarctic continent.

The Antarctic region embraces a very large area but has only a sporadic vegetation that is confined mainly to the southern tip of South America and certain subantarctic islands in the Pacific and Atlantic.

* XV. THORA MINOR. *   XVI. HERBA PARIS.

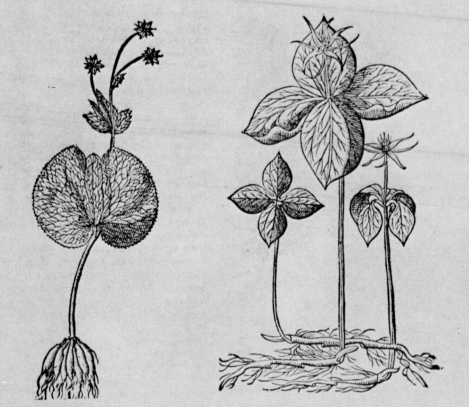

appellat: ſiquidem hæc vno tantùm conſtat caule, rotundo, duorum palmorum altitudine: è cuius medio quatuor erum- Herbæ
punt folia, eodem ambitu, crucis inſtar patentia, ſanguineæ virgæ ſimilima: alia præterea quatuor eodem modo prodeunt, delineæ
prope caulis ſummitatem, ſed hæc minima ſunt, acuta & longiuſcula: in quorum medio purpureus, vinoſuſq; extat glo-
bulus vnicus, acino ruæ ſimilis, in quo ſemen concluditur album, minutum, copioſumq̃, halicacabi modo. Radix, quæ illi
ſubeſt tenuis, in capillares ferè particulas diſſecta, palleſcit, nulla ſcorpionis caudæ effigie, nec alabaſtri modo aliqua ex
parte nitet, vt primùm Aconiti genus à Dioſcoride repræſentatur: cuius folia (vt etiam Plinius lib. 27. cap. 4. eſt author)
præterid quod cyclamino, aut cucumeri ſimilia ſunt, nunquam, quod viderim, in caulis medio ſuam habent originem,
ſed ſtatim ab ipſa radice exeunt hirſuta, humiq; recumbentia. Semen huic nullum, quod ſciam, à rei herbariæ ſcriptori-
bus redditur. Sed ex herbæ Paridis acino ſemen colligitur, cui non modo nulla deleteria vis ineſt, ſed etiam contra veneficia
præſtantiſſimum eſt medicamentum. Noui enim ego quoſdam inquit ille qui pandectas auctas edidit, quorum aliqui mor-
borum diuturnitate, atq; vero veneſiciis ſemiſtulti facti erant, hoc tantùm Paridis herbæ ſemine ad vigeſimum vſque diem
in puluerem hauſto drachmæ pondere, priſtinæ ſanitati omninò reſtitutos eſſe: id quod ego quoq̃ fateri poſſum. Baccæ
antidotis admiſcentur, quæ contra deleteria pharmaca parantur. Herba recens tuſa & illita genitalium tumores & in-
flammationes ſanat, ac pariter oculorum phlegmonas, paronychiis quoq; medetur. Herba cū baccis refrigerat & ſiccat. Prouenit

A sheet from Matthioli's herbarium (16th century) showing two medicinal plants. The need to identify such plants reliably was a strong stimulus in the development of taxonomy.

SYSTEMS OF PLANT CLASSIFICATION

Facts about plant structure, relationships, classification and nomenclature are a very important part of the science of botany. Features or characteristics of the plant (morphological characters) as well as environmental features (ecological and geographical characters) may all be used in identifying plants. They serve as an aid in evaluating similarities and differences, in the accurate description of plants and in naming plants. Detailed study of plants yields a great deal of theoretical and practical knowledge. Past centuries were characterized by the mere generalization of collected data, whereas the tendency nowadays is detailed analytical research which in terms of individual species means detailed study of the plant characters, including those of economic value. All organisms are classified according to certain rules and that is the aim and purpose of taxonomy (the branch of science dealing with the orderly classification of plants and animals) and botanical nomenclature, which determines the principles for the scientific names of plants. Taxonomy thus deals with taxons — systematic units or categories of related individuals with similar characteristics. The principal aim of taxonomy or systematics in botany is to establish a phylogenetic classification of plants based on natural evolutionary relationships, taking into consideration all the various points of view.

In the history of systematic botany there have been three time spans of unequal length in which botanists have used different criteria or methods for classifying plants. The first such period, lasting from ancient times until the eighteenth century, was a period of artificial systems. Plants were differentiated according to several prominent, arbitrarily selected characters and arranged in unnatural, artificial groups. The system worked out by Carl Linnaeus (1753) marked the peak of this period. The second period dates from approximately the beginning of the nineteenth century. This period was characterized by natural systems. Besides morphological characters, phytogeographic, palaeobotanical and ecological features were used to classify plants in natural systems which included plants of related appearance. There is no doubt that the establishment of natural systems was influenced by Charles Darwin's theory of evolution (1859), which stressed the gradual evolution and continuous change from lower, simpler forms to higher forms of life. The entire plant realm, in all its diversity, is thus a single whole and the relationships between the various groups are then much more striking. One example of a system worked out in great detail is Engler's system (1886), which gained great popularity in Europe and continues to be used with various alterations by German systematists to this day, even though its evolutionary aspect has since been refuted. In English-speaking countries the system generally used is the Bentham and Hooker system (1862—1883), but there are many more, such as the systems of A. P. De Candolle (1819), Endlicher (1836), Wettstein (1903), Bessey (1915), etc.

The 20th century marked the arrival of the third period, which has apparently reached its peak in the past several decades. It is a period of phylogenetic systems, that is systems based on natural evolutionary relationships which require the detailed and many-sided study of plants. In the opinion of some, the beginnings of this period date from the end of the 19th century with the introduction of the German system of classification in botany. New evidence is causing previous, older conclusions to be made more exact, corrected or replaced. Besides that afforded by morphology and phytogeography, particularly valuable is the information being provided by genetics, palaeontology, cytology, physiology and biochemistry. At the present time there are two leading phylogenetic systems of classification: that of Tachtadjan (1966) and that of Cronquist (1968), which are very similar. There are many more systems that take into account the evolutionary aspects based on the complex study of all characters, e. g. Benson, Emberger, Firbass, Gams, Grosgeim, Hutchinson, Melchior, Zimmermann, and others.

The following is an example of the classification of flowering plants according to Tachtadjan (the orders given as examples in parentheses refer to some of the plants depicted in the illustrated section of this book).

1. Class: Magnoliatae (Dicotyledoneae), dicotyledons
      Subclass: Magnoliidae (including the orders Magnoliales, Aristolochiales)
      Subclass: Ranunculidae (including the orders Ranunculales, Nymphaeales, Papave-
         rales)
      Subclass: Hamamelididae (including the orders Fagales, Betulales)
      Subclass: Caryophyllidae (including the large order Caryophyllales)
      Subclass: Dilleniidae (including the orders Theales, Violales, Passiflorales, Ericales,
         Primulales, Euphorbiales)
      Subclass: Rosidae (including the orders Rosales, Fabales, Nepenthales, Myrtales, Gera-
         niales)
      Subclass: Asteridae (including the orders Gentianales, Scrophulariales, Lamiales, Cam-
         panulales, Asterales)

2. Class: Liliatae (Monocotyledoneae), monocotyledons
      Subclass: Alismidae (including the orders Alismales, Potamogetonales)
      Subclass: Liliidae (including the orders Liliales, Iridales, Orchidales)
      Subclass: Commelinidae (including the orders Cyperales, Bromeliales)
      Subclass: Arecidae (including the orders Arecales, Arales, Pandanales)

The basic unit of every system of classification is the species. It is a category comprising populations of related individuals of like heredity. As a taxonomic category it may be combined with other related species to form, in ascending order, higher categories and further divided to form, in descending order, lower categories.

The principal taxonomic categories in descending order from the highest to the lowest are as follows:

The highest and most inclusive categories are kingdom, phylum and class.

The middle categories include organisms with a great number of common attributes. They are the order, family and genus. The last two are the fundamental groups which give the flora of a given region its characteristic cast.

The principal category of the lowest group is the species, a category that is often very complex and viewed and evaluated in various ways by various authorities. The taxonomic categories that rank immediately below the species are the subspecies, variety and form. In the case of cultivated plants there may also be many intergeneric hybrids (crosses between genera, as seen in orchids) and many interspecific hybrids (crosses between species). It is here that we encounter the lowest category of all — the cultivated variety or cultivar (cv.), a plant clearly distinguished by specific attributes that originated under cultivation and propagated solely by asexual, vegetative means. Hybrids are designated by the botanical names of the parent species with the letter x in between or else by placing the letter x before the new name given to the hybrid.

THE STRUCTURE OF PLANTS

Essential to the proper classification of plants, as we have already noted, is a thorough knowledge of their morphological features. First of all let us take note of the principal plant organs and their main functions. In the case of seed-bearing plants, including the flowering plants shown in the illustrated section of this book, the plant body is composed of vegetative organs

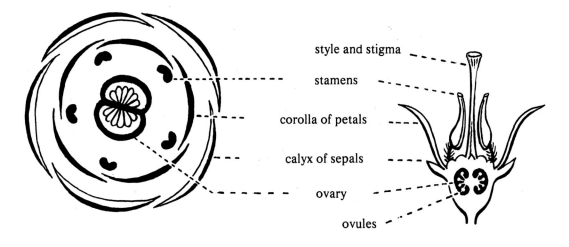

style and stigma

stamens

corolla of petals

calyx of sepals

ovary

ovules

Floral structure

(roots, stems and leaves) and reproductive organs (the stamens and pistils in the flowers). The vegetative organs may be modified in many different ways, to adapt a plant to its environment; for example the roots of aquatic plants are quite different from those of plants growing on dry land because they serve different functions.

Plants growing on dry land have underground roots that penetrate the soil and aboveground shoots differentiated into stems and leaves. The function of the roots is to anchor the plant in the soil, absorb water and minerals, and store food. The roots of floating aquatics are usually much reduced for the function of supplying the plant with food is taken over in part by the submerged stems. The roots of certain epiphytes such as bromeliads and orchids are modified as aerial roots that grow downwards until they reach the soil from which they obtain nourishment, or as holdfast roots attaching the epiphytes to their trees. In parasitic plants the roots are greatly suppressed and may be completely replaced by outgrowths called haustoria which penetrate the vascular bundles of the host plant.

There are basically two kinds of stems in landplants and plants are divided accordingly into herbaceous plants with stems that die down at the end of each growing season or woody plants with stems that form persistent woody tissue. The latter are further divided into: subshrubs with stems woody at the base and herbaceous above, shrubs with totally woody stems, and trees, which are woody plants with a single main stem that branches at the top to form a crown. An important characteristic of stems is their manner of branching. This variation is particularly striking in trees, even though it is greatly influenced by the age of the tree and its environment; much depends on whether a tree grows singly or in a stand.

The chief function of the leaves of green plants is photosynthesis. In general a leaf consists of a flat blade and stalk, or petiole. The blade may be all in one piece (simple leaf) or composed of several separate leaflets (compound leaf) and it may be parallel-veined (monocotyledons) or net-veined (dicotyledons). Leaves also differ in shape and may be variously lobed, divided, parted, cleft, etc. Of great interest are compound leaves with blade composed of several leaflets (for instance paripinnate leaves, imparipinnate leaves, etc.).

The reproductive organs of flowering plants are the male stamens and female pistils. The reproductive organs are enclosed by the protective external envelope of the flower which is called the perianth. This may be undifferentiated or else differentiated into a calyx that is usually coloured green and corolla that is usually brightly coloured and serves to attract insect pollinators. Flowers may be borne singly or in clusters — inflorescences, the two main types being racemose and cymose depending on the manner of branching. In the racemose inflorescence the lateral branches generally do not extend above the main axis and the individual flowers bloom in succession from the bottom upward or, if all are at the same level, from the margin inward towards the centre. The cymose inflorescence has a short main axis and longer lateral branches bearing flowers that bloom after the central flower. Examples of the first type of inflorescence are the raceme, panicle, spike and catkin as well as the head of clover (capitulum) and the head of composite plants (anthodium). Examples of the second type are the monochasium, dichasium, etc. The brightly coloured flowers or inflorescences of seed-bearing plants give them a beauty unequalled by any other plants and make them a constant source of interest to plant breeders and gardeners.

Further important organs vital to the further propagation of seed plants are the fruits, which contain one or more seeds. The fruit develops from the pistil, sometimes also from other parts of the flower. The fertilized ovules develop into seeds which are released if the fruits split at maturity or else remain inside and are dispersed together with the fruits. Fruits are accordingly differentiated into two main types: dehiscent, (for example follicle, legume, siliqua, capsule) and indehiscent. The latter are further differentiated into dry fruits, for example nut, achene, grain; and fleshy fruits, for example drupe (cherry, olive, almond) and berry (bilberry, currant, cucumber).

		Cymose
Racemose		

Racemose

Cymose

raceme

catkin

monochasial cyme

panicle

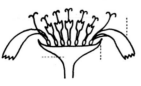

capitulum

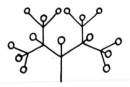

dichasial cyme

spike

anthodium

corymb

Inflorescence types

THE LANDSCAPE AND MAN

As long as man merely gathered fruits, seeds and roots he was a passive element in nature with which he was in total harmony. This method of obtaining food limited the growth of human populations for thousands of years.

The beginnings of agriculture — the cultivation of crops and domestication of the first animals — marked an enormous change in man's relation to his environment. Primitive agriculture, sowing seeds in open spaces, making use of fertile alluvial deposits, and even the first treatment (aerating) of the soil, had little effect on the look of the landscape. As time went by, however, man improved his methods of cultivation, began to expand the tracts of tilled land by felling and burning forests, established larger settlements and gradually affected and altered the look of increasingly larger areas. Man viewed plants solely in terms of their usefulness — those that were important as food, raw material for textiles, building material, etc. were cultivated, the others, those of no immediate use, became undesirable, unnecessary weeds. The areas on which the former were grown were continually expanded, the latter were purposefully suppressed.

The increase in the extent of tilled land, however, brought with it many problems. The fertile surface layers were gradually washed away from the denuded soil which had been deprived of its natural plant cover — erosion of vast areas ensued. It became necessary to replace the soil nutrients that had been used up and to eradicate the pests that spread so readily in the monocultures cultivated by man.

This long-term process reached its peak in the 20th century, in the new simplified ecosystems of the present day in which man's incursions have far exceeded the ecological tolerance of the landscape. Nature is endangered and in many parts of the world man stands on the brink of ecological catastrophe. He has created artificial habitats which are permanently maintained by him and which are totally out of tune with the natural landscape, of which the huge monoculture expanses of wheat and other crops are important examples.

The developed technology of our day provides man with unprecedented means for altering nature and extensive, rapid incursions change the look of whole landscapes. Examples of such incursions are the building of dams, transportation networks and industrial centres, the regulation of water courses along with extensive land reclamation projects, etc. All this, the result of the extremely rapid growth of the world population during the past several decades, has many adverse aspects, particularly the increasing pollution of the atmosphere and waters with a wide variety of wastes, which affects not only the life of all living organisms but also the formation of soil. In some regions man has thus become a factor whose effect far exceeds that of geological phenomena.

Man, however, has also learned a lesson from his mistakes, as indicated by examples of the thoughtful alteration of nature. Where his actions are governed by reasoning and forethought man does not exhaust the soil but increases its fertility. Remarkable results have been achieved by man in the breeding of plants, be it plant varieties with high yields or flowers of lasting quality and extraordinary beauty.

In laboratories throughout the world scientists are carrying out experiments aimed at increasing the yields of agricultural crops and thus ensuring food supplies for the present as well as future generations. At the same time the conservation of nature and natural resources is receiving more attention and concern is becoming more widespread. Most people are already aware that nature conservation is not only the 'hobby' of a small group of naturalists and nature lovers. Conservation is acquiring a new meaning — it is an essential part of man's life and activities and is aimed at preserving the essential nature of the landscape. Today it is already evident that man's very existence, his survival on Earth, depends on his solution of these problems. Preserving a certain natural balance even in the developed regions of the world gives man the certainty that he can live there. This knowledge brings with it hope for plant life as a whole and for individual plant species as well; the hope that man will prevent the disappearance and extinction of increasing numbers of species which in their diversity can never be replaced, and which in his ignorance he has endangered.

Chapter 1   FLOWERS OF SPRING

Except for the green tropical regions all parts of the world have annual seasonal changes. In the temperate to arctic zones of both hemispheres these are accompanied by changes in vegetation during the course of the year. Herbaceous plants that bloom regularly in spring have a very short growth period; many are cold-loving species that rapidly develop leaves and flowers from an underground bulb or rhizome, often before the snow has melted. The ephemeral beauty of their blossoms, striking both in terms of colour and size, is thus all the more pronounced amidst the sparse and meager spring vegetation.

Wood Anemone (1) is a plant found in shady deciduous woods throughout Europe, from Great
Anemone nemorosa L.　Britain to the central Ukraine and from the Mediterranean region to the Arctic Circle. It forms thick spreading masses resembling fresh green carpets and has trifoliate, long-stalked leaves from which rise white, starlike flowers on long stalks. The flowers are not always white — sometimes they are flushed pale violet or pale yellow.

Spring Snowflake (2) grows in shaded, damp deciduous woods, mostly beechwoods, and wet
Leucojum vernum L.　meadows from lowland to mountain districts. Its range extends from central France through central Europe southeastward to northeastern Yugoslavia and from the perialpine region to the centre of Italy.

　　The stalked flowers grow from the axils of bracts and have white perianth segments with a yellow-green spot near the tip. Not until after the flowers have faded do the strikingly large, broad leaves reach their full size to form thick, grasslike masses for a brief period.

2

3

Snowdrop (3) may often be encountered amidst patches of melting snow. The grey-green, linear
Galanthus nivalis L. leaves grow from an underground bulb and are enclosed at the base by a sheath-like scale. The erect or slightly bent stems bear solitary, drooping flowers coloured white with green spots and enclosed at first in a green, white-edged bract. The Snowdrop has a somewhat discontinuous range from the Pyrenees, western and central Europe eastward to the central Ukraine; in the south its range extends to Sicily and Greece and in the north it occurs sporadically only as far as the lower Odra region.

Oxlip (4) unlike the Cowslip (species no. 5) is generally encountered in foothills and mountains
Primula elatior (L.) — in meadows and forest margins. It forms a basal leaf rosette from
Grufb. which rises a stalk up to 30 cm long terminated by a one-sided umbel composed of several flowers. A characteristic feature is the narrow, tubular calyx pressed tightly to the corolla tube; it is pale yellow with sharp green edges and is divided almost halfway to the base into five teeth. The corolla is sulphur yellow with an orange throat and spreading lobes. This is a variable species which throughout its range occurs as several subspecies differing in the relative proportions of the leaf blade to petiole.

Cowslip (5) creates spots of colour with its pretty deep yellow flowers in rather dry meadows,
Primula veris L. open woods, woodland margins and scrub during late spring. It grows in lowland country as well as in foothills from the British Isles to the central Volga region; in the north in Scandinavia it extends to the Arctic Circle and in the south it occurs intermittently as far as southern Spain, central Italy and Greece. The stem is dotted with reddish glands and grows from a basal leaf rosette. The leaves are revolute at first and wrinkled with an undulate margin. The flower stem is terminated by a cluster of stalked flowers arranged in an umbel. The calyx, coloured

4

5

greenish-yellow, is inflated and separated from the corolla. A characteristic feature of this species is that different plants have styles of different lengths. In a single locality one will encounter individuals with long styles and ones with short styles. This arrangement, known as heterostyly, serves to prevent self-pollination.

European Dog's-tooth Violet (6)
Erythronium dens-canis L.

generally grows in beechwoods and on shrubby hillsides in hilly country, chiefly on basic rock substrates such as limestone. The ovoid bulb bears an erect stem with two purplish-spotted leaves that narrow into a sheath-like stalk. The stem is terminated by a large solitary flower with backward-pointing petals spotted on the outside and with a small notch at the base. This plant may be encountered from central Europe and Czechoslovakia southward to the Mediterranean region — to the central section of the Iberian and Apennine Peninsulas and through the Balkan Peninsula northeastward to the western Ukraine.

Two-leaved Squill (7)
Scilla bifolia L.

generally grows in damp woodland and may also be found in damp meadows in lowland as well as mountain districts. In Europe it has a continuous distribution from southern France through the central and southern part of the continent to the central Ukraine. The underground bulb bears a stem with two fresh green leaves. The flower stalk is terminated by a raceme of stalked flowers. This is a variable species particularly as regards the number of flowers in the inflorescence, caused by differing environmental conditions.

30

6

7

8

9

Heath Anemone (8) has both the stem and stem leaves covered thickly with spreading hairs.
Pulsatilla patens (L.) Mill. The solitary flowers are large, open, upright, pale blue-violet and likewise hairy outside. The long-stalked leaves develop after the flowers are spent and they die down for the winter. Heath Anemones are distributed from central Europe to the steppe regions of the USSR, their range extending as far as the central Urals.

Meadow Anemone (9) grows on open grassy hillsides, particularly on volcanic substrates. Its
Pulsatilla pratensis (L.) Mill. subsp. *nigricans* (Störk) Asch.-Graeb. striking pendent flowers are blackish-violet and thickly covered with silky hairs as are the stem and leaves.

Uvularia grandiflora Smith (10) grows on the Atlantic coast of North America, mostly in woodland communities. The flowers are drooping, bell-like, up to 5 cm long and open either singly or in twos. The stem is leafless at the bottom; the upper half is covered with alternate, sessile leaves that are elliptic and pointed. Some species of the genus *Uvularia* are grown as ornamentals.

10

11

Silverweed (11) is a common species of nitrogen-rich situations, such as village greens, way-
Potentilla anserina L. sides, and the margins of ponds, streams and rivers; it often grows
along roadsides, spreading from lowland to mountain districts. It is
distinguished by creeping stems, sometimes more than a metre long,
with basal rosettes of odd-pinnate leaves divided into deeply serrate
leaflets; the latter are silvery silky-white-felted beneath. The flowers
grow on long stalks from the axils of the leaves; they are large and
coloured golden yellow. This species is found throughout the whole
northern hemisphere, extending as far as the Arctic Circle. It was used
in folk medicine to treat inflammatory diseases.

Spring Cinquefoil (12) is a plant of sunny, grassy as well as stony slopes and woodland margins
Potentilla
tabernaemontani
Aschers.
and is also found in dry hedgerows, sandy pastureland and forest clearings in lowland and hilly districts. In all these places it forms thick, continuous carpets that spread by means of rooting shoots. The underground rhizome bears basal leaf rosettes from the centre of which rise numerous prostrate, prominently branched stems. The palmate leaves are composed of narrow wedge-shaped leaflets, covered with shining hairs and with serrate margins. The golden-yellow flowers are borne on short stalks and have broad notched petals with narrow sepals. A characteristic feature of this species is the enlarged cup-like floral receptacle, the hypanthium, formed by the union of the lower parts of the floral envelopes. Spring Cinquefoil is found in western and central Europe northward to southern Sweden.

12

White Butterbur (13) appears in spring on ground that is still bare, without any trace of other
Petasites albus (L.)   green vegetation. It is usually found by the wayside, in roadside ditches,
Gaertn.   on gravelly embankments and in the mountains beside mountain
streams and springs. The thick creeping rhizome bears flowering stems
covered with pale green scales. The terminal raceme consists of heads
of yellowish-white flowers with long stigmas. The underside of the
basal leaves, which appear after the flowers fade, is covered with thick
white wool.

Winter Aconite (14) forms short stems with a whorl of leaves beneath the single terminal
Eranthis hyemalis   flower composed of a coloured calyx and corolla modified into glands.
(L.) Salisb.   The basal leaves, which are long-stalked, appear after the flowers have
faded but are soon covered by the vegetation of later spring-flowering
species. Winter Aconite is very hardy and often grows up through
a thin layer of snow. It grows in broad-leaved woods in the Mediterranean region of southeastern Europe and often becomes naturalized in
central and western Europe.

Lesser Celandine (15) is a plant of wet, muddy soils and damp, shaded places in scrub. It may be
Ranunculus ficaria   found at various elevations. It has large, club-shaped tubers which bear
L. subsp. *bulbifer*   stiff, glossy, stalked leaves, shaped like rounded kidneys. The flowering
(Marsden-Jones)   stems bear solitary, stalked flowers with glossy golden-yellow petals.
Lawalrée   Tiny ovoid bulbils are formed in the axils of the lower leaves.

13

14

Sweet Woodruff (16) is a typical plant of shady beechwoods and open oak-hornbeam woods,
Galium odoratum chiefly in lowland and hilly districts, though it is also found in mountain
(L.) Scop. regions. It is distributed throughout the whole northern hemisphere. It
always occurs in large numbers and forms large, spreading carpets. The
stem is erect, four-angled, glabrous and covered with whorls of six to
nine leaves; the lower leaves are broadly oblong, the upper leaves
lanceolate, with rough margins and sharp tips. The flowers are ar-

15

ranged in dense terminal panicles and have a white funnel-shaped corolla divided almost halfway to the base into four spreading lobes. Noteworthy is the fruit, which is covered with hooked bristles. Sweet Woodruff was formerly used in folk medicine. It contains high concentrations of aromatic coumarin and the extract from the plant was added to herb liqueurs and wines, for instance Germany's traditional 'Maibowle'. There are numerous species of the genus *Galium* with very variable ecological requirements — most grow on rocky sunny slopes and resemble xerophilous plants.

Field Mouse-ear (17) is a common species of dry meadows, pastures, grassy hedgerows and
Cerastium arvense L. stony overgrown slopes (it is also found in rock gardens) from lowland to high mountain elevations. Because of its great vertical range lowland and mountain populations have different characteristics and the plants are sometimes evaluated as separate subspecies or even different species. The conspicuous terminal inflorescences are composed of

16

17

five to fifteen flowers up to 2 cm in diameter with a white, funnel-shaped corolla which is much longer than the downy calyx. The plant is loosely tufted with numerous semi-creeping to ascending stems and many sterile leaf rosettes — it is readily identified even when not in flower.

Bulbous Fumewort (18) grows in damp leafy soils in open woods where it is often found near streams. The relatively large flowers have a long recurved spur. Bulbous Fumewort is distributed from the Rhine region eastward to the central Ukraine (Don River region) and north to Denmark and southern Sweden. In the Mediterranean region it is scattered throughout northwestern Spain, throughout all of Italy and from the Balkans to Macedonia and Bulgaria.

Corydalis cava (L.) Schw.-Koerte

18

19

Almond (19) is partial to sunny, shrubby and rocky slopes and vineyards with rich loess soil. It
Amygdalus nana L. forms densely-leaved, semi-creeping shrubs with shining branches
(syn. *Prunus tenella* which are tinged with silver in older specimens. The leaves are almost
Batsch.) sessile, elliptic, with wedge-shaped bases, pointed tips and sharply serrate margins. The flowers open before the leaves in March and April.
They grow on short twigs (brachyblasts) either singly or in twos or
threes. The enlarged fleshy receptacle (hypanthium) is cup-shaped. The
fruit is a globose, yellow-grey, felted drupe. The outer cover (pericarp)
is leathery and encloses a furrowed seed. This shrub is distributed
throughout the northern hemisphere from the Pacific coast to central
North America and in the Old World from central Europe to eastern
Asia. This almond is closely related to the Common Almond (*A.
communis* L. syn. *P. dulcis* Mill.) which is distributed from Europe's
Mediterranean region to central Asia and which has been grown since
time immemorial for its edible seeds — 'sweet almonds'. Besides 'sweet
almonds' there are also 'bitter almonds' but these are the seeds of another variety of the Common Almond; they are poisonous and contain
a bitter volatile oil.

Magnolia hypoleuca Sieb. et Zucc. (20) is native to Japan. The young twigs are silky-felted, the
leaves deciduous, obovate, and rounded at the tip. The flowers, up to
6 cm across, are solitary and appear on the twigs at the same time as
the leaves. The outer perianth segments are green, the inner segments

21

rose-tinted or white. An important characteristic is the spiral arrangement of the carpels on the conical receptacle. The carpels develop into separate, dehiscent, many-seeded follicles. Collectively they form an aggregate fruit — a cone. This species belongs to a genus named after the French botanist Pierre Magnol and comprises some 30 species worldwide. Some are deciduous, others evergreen, and they are distributed chiefly in eastern Asia and North America. Some are popularly grown as ornamentals for their huge flowers in parks and gardens throughout the temperate and Mediterranean regions of Europe. Noteworthy is the fact that in past geological periods these woody plants occupied a wide range, occurring, for instance, in Iceland, Greenland, Alaska, and even in the southern hemisphere, in Australia.

Lily-of-the-valley (21)
Convallaria majalis L.
usually has two broadly elliptic leaves that grow from a creeping, branched rhizome. These leaves are furled and encased by sheath-like scales at the base when they first appear above the ground. The flowering stem is erect and terminated by a loose raceme of milky white or rose-tinted flowers. These are stalked, drooping, and bell-shaped with a pleasant fragrance. The perianth has short spreading lobes, the stam-

ens have bright yellow anthers. The fruit is a red berry. The seeds contain important toxic substances used in the preparation of medicines for stimulating heart activity. The plant may be found throughout all Europe to the Urals and from the northern part of the Mediterranean region to the Arctic Circle. It has also been introduced to the eastern coast of North America. In the Far East, including Japan, its place is taken by a closely related species. A characteristic of Lilies-of-the-valley is that they form extensive masses that spread by vegetative means but generally do not flower.

Hairy Violet (22) is a plant of dry, sunny slopes, pastures, open woods and woodland margins; it
Viola hirta L. may even grow on wet loamy soils. It forms a short, polycephalous, underground rhizome which bears a thick rosette of basal leaves in the spring. There is no stem above ground. The blades of these spring leaves are conspicuously triangular with heart-shaped bases and finely crenate margins whereas the summer leaves are much larger and usually longish ovate. The flower stalks, terminated by unscented flowers, rise directly from the leaf rosette. The sepals are blunt, the petals notched and pale blue-violet with a curved, reddish-violet spur. This violet is very easily identified by the hairy stipules at the base of the leaf stalks, which are particularly conspicuous in spring.

22

23

24

44

Wood Violet (23) occurs in woodland communities at various altitudes and is characterized by
Viola sylvatica Fries. a short underground rhizome. On the surface it forms a basal rosette of long-stalked leaves that are heart-shaped in outline with pointed tips and hairs on the upper side. From the centre of the rosette rises a leafy stem branching at the base and terminated by long-stalked flowers. These are pendent, unscented, with narrow, pointed sepals, narrowly-ovate petals and a characteristic straight, pointed spur. Important organs from the systematic viewpoint are the stipules at the base of the leaf stalks for the genus *Viola* includes a great many very similar species that readily interbreed. The shape and margins of the stipules provide an easy means of identification. Besides the wild violets there are also many cultivated varieties, so-called pansies. These are probably the hybrid offspring of several Asian species, many of which flower twice a year producing a great variety of forms. All species of violets growing in the wild are very tolerant of varying environmental conditions (heat, moisture and altitude), but they are mostly found on acidic rock substrates.

Ramsons (24) forms large masses in shady, damp flood plain forests beside woodland streams
Allium ursinum L. from lowland to dwarf pine elevations. The underground bulb bears two broad, elliptic basal leaves, up to 10 cm long, that taper into a stalk, and a rounded, leafless stem terminated by a whitish spathe from which the inflorescence grows — a globose umbel composed of tiny stalked flowers. The perianth segments are linear and spreading. Ramsons is

25

distributed throughout all western, central and southern Europe, its range extending southward to Sicily and Greece. Like other members of the genus *Allium* it has a typical aroma and its presence can readily be identified by the sense of smell.

Forsythia suspensa (Thunb.) Vahl (25) is a shrub with hollow, four-angled, warty stems covered with simple, opposite leaves. The flowers appear before the leaves on short axillary shoots. The corollas are bell-like and deeply divided into spreading lobes. The sepals are short and coloured green. The fruit is a warty capsule. This species is native to China where it reaches a height of three metres; it includes many ornamental varieties popularly grown in parks. It is interesting to note that the genus *Forsythia* is distributed in the Far East and only one species, *F. europaea*, grows in Albania. The European species is no doubt a remnant of the Tertiary flora.

Nine-leaved Toothwort (26) is a spring-flowering plant found in beechwoods, where in shaded,
Dentaria leafy soil it often forms spreading carpets. The stout, creeping rhizome
enneaphyllos L. bears simple, unbranched stems with whorls of three leaves at the top. The flowers, arranged in a raceme, are short-stalked, pendent, and col-

26

27

oured pale yellow. A characteristic feature are the fruits — linear sili-
quas with glossy seeds. When spring draws to a close the whole plant
dries and dies down, disappearing from the forest's herb layer until the
following spring.

Asarabacca (27) is a herb with a creeping, branched rhizome from which rises a short, ascend-
Asarum europaeum L. ing stem covered with scales and hairs and bearing two to four long-
stalked leaves at the top. The leaves are orbicular in outline, leathery,
dark green above and a paler green on the underside, with a deeply cut,
heart-shaped base. The flowers are unusual, solitary, short-stalked,
drooping and smell strongly of pepper. They are covered by the leaves
so that they readily escape notice when viewed from above. The three
perianth segments are pointed, brownish outside and dark violet within.
The scientific name of this plant is derived from the Greek word *asa-*

28

ros, meaning carpet, because the plant forms spreading masses in damp, shaded woodland soil. The species is distributed throughout all Europe and in Asia extends to central Siberia. The genus *Asarum* is found only in the northern hemisphere, chiefly in North America.

Spring Pheasant's Eye (28) is a thermophilous and xerophilous species and so it favours grassy
Adonis vernalis L. slopes and stony steppes. It also grows in open oak stands, particularly on volcanic rock substrates and loess soils. The flowers, up to 8 cm in diameter, have a greater number of petals than sepals and a calyx that is covered with soft hairs. Spring Pheasant's Eye is distributed throughout all central and eastern Europe, extending from there through the Urals to the upper reaches of the Yenisei River. It is one of the perennial members of the genus, which includes many related annual species with red or violet-red flowers usually growing as weeds in fields.

Common Lungwort (29) bears terminal cymes of short-stalked flowers at the top of the flowering leafy stems in spring. The petals are pink at first, violet in full bloom and bluish after pollination. A characteristic feature are the tufts of hairs inside the corolla tube. Prominent features in summer are the dense basal rosettes of long-stalked leaves. Common Lungwort is generally found in leafy soil in mixed, broad-leaved woods, chiefly oak-hornbeam woods, and has a continuous distribution from the Rhine region throughout all Europe to western Siberia.

Pulmonaria officinalis L.

Noble Liverleaf (30) is found chiefly in shady or faintly sun-dappled broad-leaved woods. It has a creeping underground rhizome which bears a stem resembling a flower stalk and covered with spreading hairs. The leaves are of two kinds: long-stalked basal leaves that are three-lobed with a heart-

Hepatica nobilis Schreber

29

shaped base and a softly, hairy undersurface; and stem leaves that are small with an entire margin, arranged in a whorl of three immediately below the flower so that they resemble a calyx. The flowers are large, open, dark or pale violet, very occasionally deep pink or white, and always with a large number of perianth segments. Noble Liverleaf grows in Europe from Spain to the central Ukraine and has related species in the eastern part of North America, Japan and the western Himalayas. It was formerly used in folk medicine to treat liver diseases and hence its generic name in Latin. It is one of the first spring flowering herbs in the places where it grows, for the herbaceous vegetation of woods develops somewhat later than that of meadows.

Coltsfoot (31) is a pioneer plant in places where a new plant cover is being formed and is also *Tussilago farfara* L. found in places affected by the inroads of civilization, sometimes even in waste places. It is common, for example, in grassland, on embankments, in hedgerows and in clearings, being partial to damp, clay soils. It has a creeping rhizome which bears scaly, unbranched stems terminated by solitary heads of golden-yellow flowers. The involucral bracts beneath the flower head are green, sometimes flushed with red. The flower heads glow brightly, sometimes as early as late February, when other plants are just beginning their growth. After the flowers are spent the stems increase in length and bend towards the ground. It is at this time that the striking orbicular leaves, each with a heart-shaped base, appear; they are usually toothed on the margins, pale green above and grey, with a felty texture on the underside. The medicinal properties of this plant have been known since time immemorial, particularly in the treatment of diseases of the upper respiratory passages. This species may be encountered throughout all Europe and Asia.

31

Bog Heather or Cross-leaved Heath (32) is a shrubby plant found in pine woods and wet
Erica tetralix L. heaths throughout western Europe. The leaves, arranged in whorls, are
linear, prickly and persistent. The flowers are arranged in dense umbel-
like clusters and have a characteristic, flask-shaped (urceolate) corolla.

Spring Vetchling (33) with its brightly coloured flowers immediately catches the eye in the
Lathyrus vernus (L.) open broad-leaved woods and woodland margins where it grows. It
Bernh. (syn. *Orobus* favours calcareous loess soils but also does well on acidic rock sub-
vernus L.) strates from lowland to foothill districts. It has a continuous distribution in Europe from the Pyrenees across the whole continent, extending beyond the Urals to the upper reaches of the Yenisei River. In
Europe it is a common species in the Mediterranean region and in the
north it extends along the coast of Norway to the Arctic Circle. The
stems of this vetchling are erect, unbranched and glabrous. The leaves,

51

borne in the upper half of the stems, are composed of three pairs of leaflets and their rachis terminates in a point. The individual leaflets are ovate and long-pointed, the uppermost leaflets are usually narrow. Most of the leaves appear after the flowers have faded. The flowers are large and arranged in scanty, long-stalked racemes. The flower is typical of the pea family to which the plant belongs; the largest upper petal (standard) is round and recurved, the two lateral petals (wings) are smaller and wide and the two lower petals are fused by their lower edges (keel). The genus *Lathyrus* includes more than 100 species, most of which have the terminal, odd leaflet modified into a tendril; these species are grown as ornamentals, particularly for their beautifully coloured and fragrant flowers.

Marsh Marigold (34) is a plant with specific ecological requirements and that is why it grows
Caltha palustris L.   only in damp and muddy situations, beside streams, on the edges of ponds and in wet meadows, from lowland to mountain districts. It has a persistent sparsely-branched stem that is sometimes prostrate with roots in the ground. The basal leaves are stalked, large and heart-shaped, the upper leaves sessile and kidney-shaped. All have crenate or entire margins in spring, whereas in summer they are sharply dentate. The flowers are borne singly on long stalks and have shining perianth segments, usually coloured yellow but sometimes white. The fruits, splitting follicles, are curved and narrow into a long beak. This species

34

35

is distributed throughout all of North America and Eurasia. It often occurs at high mountain elevations and in cold northern regions, nearly to 80° latitude North. The genus *Caltha* includes some 40 species, 12 of them distributed in the colder regions of the southern hemisphere. All the species contain poisonous substances.

Green Hellebore (35)
Helleborus viridis L.
has a leafless, red-spotted stem that is sparsely-branched and glabrous for most of its length but hairy at the top. The basal leaves die down for the winter; they are long-stalked and divided into narrowly lanceolate segments with serrate margins. The upper surface is dark green, often pruinose with recessed veins, the underside is pale and hairy with prominent veins. The occasional stem leaves, if produced, are divided

into five segments. The flowers are pendent and long-stalked; the corolla is yellow-green and funnel-trumpet-shaped with a revolute margin, the sepals are green and wide. Many related species of the genus *Helleborus* have violet-purple flowers that appear in spring. The Green Hellebore is probably native to southwestern Europe and is distributed from the British Isles to central Europe southward to Spain and northern Italy.

Upright Clematis (36) is a non-climbing plant with stems that become woody from the base. It
Clematis recta L.   grows in open woods and on shrubby slopes, being partial to limestone and volcanic rock substrates. The bottom stem leaves are undivided whereas those growing on the upper half of the stem are odd-pinnate and composed of stalked leaflets that are hairy on the underside. The flowers, arranged in dense terminal inflorescences, have a white calyx with a felted margin and no petals. A characteristic feature are the fruits which have long hairy appendages. Upright Clematis is distributed throughout all central, southeastern and eastern Europe; many related climbing species are grown as ornamentals in gardens, quite a few of them escaping and naturalizing readily in the wild.

36

Chapter 2   CACTI AND OTHER SUCCULENTS

The dry regions of the world, which have little underground water and insufficient rainfall with high temperatures and long hours of sunlight, are inhabited by xerophilous plants that are adapted to life in these uncongenial conditions. They are capable of surviving long periods of drought by absorbing and storing water during the rainy season and using it economically for their life processes, chiefly by limiting surface evaporation. The unusual structure of the internal tissues enables them to withstand dry conditions better than other plants. The aboveground parts have a very low surface area to volume ratio and hence the least possible exposure to and contact with the atmosphere. Instead of being flat and spreading the leaves are needle-like or scale-like. The top parts are also enlarged and fleshy, another adaptation to increase the proportion of body mass to surface area and designed to conserve moisture; that is why these plants are called succulents (the Latin word *succus* means juice, sap).

Cacti are without doubt the principal and largest group of succulents. Native to the Americas they are distributed from British Columbia, where the species *Opuntia missouriensis* grows as far north as 53° North, to Patagonia in Argentina, where the species *Opuntia australis* extends to 52° South. Only occasionally are these plants found elsewhere than in the Americas. Long before the discovery of the New World by Europeans, cacti such as opuntias were grown by the native Indians chiefly for their tasty, succulent fruits.

Other important succulents are the plants of the spurge (Euphorbiaceae) family, which developed in the tropics of the Old World in conditions similar to those of the cacti in America and hence have a similar structure. They include annual species as well as perennial herbs, subshrubs and trees. They are distributed north and south of the equator mostly in Africa and Asia; woody types grow in the tropics whereas most of the herbaceous species are to be found in the temperate regions.

A third group of succulents are the plants of the family Mesembryanthemaceae. The name is derived from the Greek word *mesembriá,* meaning midday, because the plants bloom in full

38

39

58

41

sunlight. They have fleshy leaves and stems, or only basal leaves. Found in dry to desert regions, they are amongst the most peculiar of plants. They often resemble pebbles in size, shape and colouration — examples of plant 'mimicry'. Most interesting are the species that consist of only two fleshy, opposite, basal leaves not at all reminiscent of leaves as we know them. For instance in the genus *Lithops* and *Conophytum* the two leaves are joined along their entire length and resemble a column, upside-down cone, pear or fig. The flowers are prominently star-like and reminiscent of the flower heads of composite plants; they are usually coloured white, yellow or violet. The plants' superb blending with their environment is a response to the arid conditions of the South African deserts and does not appear to be a protective device designed to keep them from being eaten by animals since their flowers are large and strikingly coloured.

We thus find succulent plants in two separate parts of the world — in Africa and the Americas — where they evolved under like conditions and often developed practically the same forms. Whereas Africa has a great many succulents ranging from treelike spurges to tiny pebble-like mesembryanthemums and including the plants of the carpetweed (Asclepiadaceae) family, America boasts the large family of succulents — the cacti, ranging from 15-metre-high specimens to tiny balls only 1 cm in diameter. Found in both regions are the succulent plants of the stonecrop (Crassulaceae) family.

Selenicereus urbanianus (Gürcke et Wgt.) Br. et R. (37) is a species native to the Caribbean islands of Cuba and Haiti where it flowers in the warm, fragrant tropical nights. Its huge blossoms, up to 25 cm across in full bloom, have

59

42 43

earned it the name 'Queen of the Night'. The outer perianth segments
are striking, being long, narrow and spread out like a star, thus making
the flower look extremely exotic. This species has long, slender stems
often furnished with aerial roots. Though the flowers of this cactus are
extraordinarily large they disappear in the daytime, rapidly wilting and
drying up in the heat of the tropical sun.

Lobivia rossii Böd. (38) belongs to a very large genus numbering more than 100 species found
in the upland plateaux of central Bolivia. All are noted for the extraordinary variability of colouration of their flowers. *L. rossii* includes
a great many varieties ranging in colour from pale yellow to carmine
red. Shown in the illustration is *L. rossii* var. *salmonea* Backbg. which
has wine-red flowers with a corolla tube up to 4 cm long. These are
borne singly at the top of a rounded stem approximately 8 cm in diameter. The surface of the plant is covered with white stellate spines up
to 1.5 cm long.

Lobivia famatimensis (Speg.) Br. et R. (39) is a miniature cactus approximately 3.5 cm high
with strikingly large, bright flowers ranging from yellow to red and
prominent small spines pressed tightly to the stem. The plant is named
after the Famatima Mountains in northern Argentina where it grows at
elevations of 2,000 to 3,000 metres.

Lophophora williamsii (Lem.) Coult. (40) has a grey-green, rounded stem with ribs that are sometimes divided into tubercles. Growing from the areoles at the tips of the tubercles are tufts of stiff matted hairs forming a thick cover of greyish-yellow wool on the crown. The flowers are small, 2 to 3 cm long and tinted pink, violet or yellow; they are produced throughout the whole growing period. The fruits are soft, club-shaped berries containing black seeds up to 1.5 mm long. *L. williamsii,* native to northern Mexico, is well-known for its narcotic properties, as are other species of this genus. Indians of the Chichimeca tribe used the extract from the roots of several species of *Lophophora* (they called the roots *peyote*) in place of wine to become inebriated; the state of 'intoxication' was very brief and without visible after-effects. The cult of *Lophophora* cacti gradually declined with the advent of the white men and their liquor, a far more potent substitute for the so-called miraculous cactus root.

Hamatocactus hamatacanthus (Mühlpfrdt.) Knuth (41) is a globose cactus which reaches a length of 60 cm when fully grown. An interesting feature is the single spine growing from the centre of the radiating spines at the tip of each tubercle. It is elastic, hooked, and up to 12 cm long — much longer than the other spines. The flowers form a broad funnel, approximately 7 cm long, in which the throat is a different colour from the petals. This species may be encountered in the stony semidesert regions on the border separating the United States and Mexico, where succulent cacti are very common.

44

45

46

Ferocactus victoriensis (Rose) Backbg. (42) is named after the Mexican city Ciudad Victoria, where it was first discovered and described. It is only 15 cm high, making it one of the smallest members of the genus *Ferocactus,* which includes columnar species up to 4 metres high. Great variability in height is a characteristic feature of this genus; besides the aforementioned columnar cacti, which measure up to 80 cm in diameter and weigh several tons, it embraces small, globose species that form continuous cushions. Another distinguishing characteristic of the genus, whose members are distributed from Utah and Nevada in the U.S.A. to northern Mexico, are relatively small flowers, generally coloured yellow or red. It may be said that their diversity of form demonstrates the remarkable morphological adaptability of these succulents.

Ariocarpus lloydii Rose (43) was not discovered until 1911 on the parched stony hillsides of northern Mexico, despite its large size (its clumps measure up to 75 cm across). It has huge, turnip-like underground roots and a body composed of hard, pointed tubercles or furrowed mammillae arranged in a rosette. Between these mammillae are striking white or yellowish trichomes forming a stiff terminal crest from which rise the relatively large flowers. The fruit is a berry containing black seeds up to 1.5 mm long.

Sulcorebutia arenacea (Card.) Ritt. (44) is a 'dwarf' amongst cacti for its globose body reaches a height of less than 4 cm. It is covered with white spines, approximately 5 mm long, arranged in a spiral. The striking flowers are borne near the top of the cactus so that they overtop the body. This species is

rightfully considered a miniature gem that brightens the greyish-brown, stony, high mountain semidesert regions of the Bolivian altiplano. It belongs to a genus that numbers some 18 species widespread in north-eastern Bolivia in the neighbourhood of the city of Cochabamba at elevations above 4,000 metres. Members of this genus are distinguished by extremely long areoles.

Mammillaria parkinsonii Ehrenbg. (45), a native of Mexico, is an extremely variable species embracing a great many varieties. Growing from the areoles on the globose body, up to 15 cm high, are two types of spines: short, stellate spines pressed close to the body and stiff, whitish to reddish spines nearly 4 cm long. The perianth is brownish-pink with a creamy margin.

Mammillaria solisioides Backbg. (46) is a minute plant up to 1 cm high but with yellow-white flowers more than 2 cm long. Particularly striking are the delicate, radial, overlapping spines which make this miniature cactus look slightly larger than it actually is. This cactus is found in Central America and belongs to a genus that numbers some 100 species distributed from California through Central America to northern Colombia. Some species are also found on the Lesser Antilles in the Caribbean. Mammillarias generally have relatively small bodies covered with rows of mammillae with flowers growing from the axils. These form a ring at the top of the usually ovoid stem. Older specimens bear several rings of flowers, one above the other.

Mammillaria centricirrha Lem. (47) is native to Mexico. It has green stems covered with white wool at the top and reaching a height of 12 cm; it may be up to 20 cm in diameter. The flowers, which are small, up to 2.5 cm across and coloured carmine-red, are set amidst prominent spines.

Mammillaria crucigera Mart. (48) is a species with cylindrical to ovoid stems, thickly covered with pale green, conical spines about 5 mm long. It is found in Mexico.

Mammillaria herrerae Werd. (49) grows in the Mexican mountain districts of Querétaro and Cadereyta. The globose body of this cactus is very small — about 3.5 cm in diameter. An attractive ornamental feature are delicate spines growing from the warty tubercles and reaching a length of up to 5 mm. The fruits are carmine-red berries and contain black seeds.

Pseudolobivia longispina (Br. et R.) Backbg. (50) is an Argentine-Bolivian species that grows in the parched barren highlands of this region. The stem is globose, up to 25 cm in diameter and covered with spines that are 8 cm long and hooked at first but straightening at maturity. Cacti of the genus *Pseudolobivia* resemble lobivias (species no. 38, 39) in habit of growth and arrangement of the ribs and spines but differ chiefly by having smaller flowers with a longer corolla tube.

49

50

Thelocactus leucacanthus (Zucc.) Br. et R. (51) is native to the mountains of northern Mexico where there are several varieties, differing in the colour of the flowers. The cylindrical body is about 15 cm high and covered with relatively large spines, coloured brownish or reddish at the base. The illustrated species belongs to the variety *schmollii* Werd. with flowers about 4 cm long and broadly funnel-shaped.

Pelecyphora pseudopectinata Backbg. (52) occurs very occasionally on the semidry, shrubby, and stony slopes and tablelands of northern Mexico. It is a tiny globose cactus approximately 6 cm high and almost 5 cm in diameter. The surface is covered with small tubercles regularly arranged in longitudinal ribs and bearing short, stiff, comb-like spines that create the impression of a neatly-spread whitish web. The regularity of this network is underscored by the vertical ribs on the body surface. The flowers are pale pink, sessile, and borne singly on the spiny tubercles; the inner, coloured perianth segments have a prominent reddish-brown vein down the centre.

Gymnocalycium uruguayense (Ar.) Br. et R. (53) is distinguished by marked variability in the length and shape of the spines, which resemble the long legs of a spider. The specific name indicates that it is found in Uruguay. It belongs to a genus of cacti marked by extraordinary diversity in general appearance as well as in the shape and colour of the flowers. There are about 150 species of the genus *Gymnocalycium,* distributed from the northern boundary of Patagonia through most of Argentina to Uruguay and Paraguay, extending as far as southern Brazil and Bolivia.

51

52

53

54

Gymnocalycium carminanthum Backbg. (54) is found in Argentina. It is distinguished by its globose shape and notably by the gleaming white, appressed spines on the tuberculate ribs. Particularly striking is the apex of the body with its relatively large spines of varying length.

Submatucana currundayensis (Ritt.) Backbg. (55) was named after the region where it grows, the mountain district of Cerro Currunday in the Andes of northeastern Peru, where it occurs at elevations above 3,000 metres. It is a globose cactus barely 15 cm high covered with yellow-brown spines 3.5 cm long. A characteristic feature of the flower is the long corolla tube covered with short ciliae outside.

Neolloydia gielsdorfiana (Werd.) F. M. Knuth (56) grows in the mountain districts of Mexico. It (syn. *Gymnocactus* is a small, globose cactus reaching a maximum height of 15 cm. A de-
gielsdorfianus (Werd.) corative feature are the areoles tipped with white felt and bearing long,
Backbg.) curved spines forming a star-like pattern; the spines arc pale brown

with black tips. The flowers are gleaming white, about 2.5 cm across and rise from the continuous white-felted cover which is thicker at the top of the body.

Aztekium ritteri (Böd.) Böd. (57) is a small plant with a distinctive body. It has deep grooves parallel to the main ribs which are covered with areoles and crosswise grooves between the main ribs. Growing from the tubercled areoles are minute spines interspersed with gleaming white flowers only 8 mm across. This cactus grows in Mexico's Nuevo León district.

Rebutia senilis Backbg. (58) is a tiny globose cactus found on the practically inaccessible ridges of the South American Andes in northwestern Argentina. The stems of this species are up to 8 cm high and 6 to 7 cm across. The flowers are striking, approximately 5 cm long, 4 cm wide and coloured carmine red. This species includes many varieties differing in the colour of the flowers (from pink through red, yellow to violet) and in the kind of spines, which may be short or long and glassy-white or yellow-brown to black.

55

56

57

Cleistocactus tominensis (Wgt.) Backbg. (59) is an erect cactus about 2 metres high named after the Bolivian valley Tomina, located east of the city of Sucre about 2,000 metres above sea level. The flowers, which are about 3 cm long, protrude from the long, lateral branches which are a characteristic feature of this species. These branches also bear areoles which are thickly covered with yellowish spines.

Opuntia chakensis Speg. (60) is a tree-like, little-branched cactus, generally without spines or only one or two spines growing from the areoles. As the specific name indicates, it is native to the lowlands and hill country of the southern and northern Chaco region of northern Argentina and western Paraguay.

58

59

Obregonia denegri Frič (61) is the only member of the genus *Obregonia*. It is a moderately large cactus. The body is covered with ribs composed of three-sided protuberances bearing flowers about 2.5 cm across.

Melocactus harlowii (Br. et R.) Vpl. (62) is an endemic species of eastern Cuba. The stem is globose or cylindrical and topped when fully grown by a felted, long-cylindrical 'head' bearing rosy-red flowers about 2 cm across. The 'head' is about 8 cm high and covered with tiny spines arranged in groups of four. Besides these there are also tufts of spines growing from the areoles covering the stem. It is interesting to note that this species belongs to the genus of cacti that were the first to be discovered in the New World and were called 'spiny melons'.

60

61

62

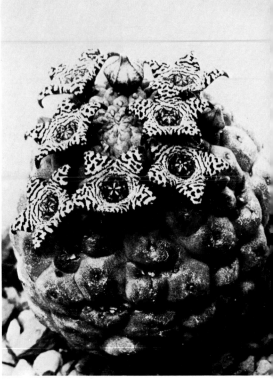

63

Trichocaulon cactiforme N.E.Br. (63) is a succulent species widespread in southern and southwestern Africa. The stem is cylindrical, up to 15 cm high and covered with four- to six-angled, spineless tubercles. The flowers appear on the upper part of the stem and have a five-lobed, bell-like corolla 10 to 13 mm in diameter. The petals are pale yellow with reddish-brown spots.

Stapelia hirsuta L. (64) has pale green, winged stems up to 25 cm long and nearly 3 cm thick. The flowers, up to 35 cm long, are yellow striped with red and have long pointed lobes covered with purplish-red hairs.

Stapelia grandiflora Mass. (65) is a South African succulent known since the late 18th century. It has three- to four-angled stems about 20 cm high. The edges are compressed and toothed with tiny, deciduous, scale-like leaves. The striking flowers, which emerge at the base of new shoots, are usually solitary, up to 15 cm across, dark purple and thickly covered with soft, brownish-red hairs. This species resembles cacti in habit. The genus *Stapelia* includes approximately 120 South African species.

74

65

Conophytum pillansii Lovis (66) is a succulent species widespread in the stony semideserts of South Africa. The body is barely 2 cm high and ovoid. The single flower grows from a shallow fissure at the top of the stem. The plant, which is definitely xerophilous in structure, resembles a tiny pebble and is practically indistinguishable, so well does it merge with its surroundings.

Fenestraria rhopalophylla (Schltr. et Diels) N. E. Br. (67) is a South African succulent with short, club-shaped leaves 2 to 3 cm long with translucent 'windows' on the upper surface, hence the generic name derived from the Latin word *fenestra*, meaning window. The flowers resemble the flower heads of composite plants and have stalks up to 7 cm long.

66

Faucaria bosscheana (Berger) Schwant. (68) has glossy green leaves that are broadly rhomboid or lanceolate in outline with a curved tip and an irregularly toothed margin covered with white spines. The surface is covered with glandular hairs containing water that glitter in the sun like small crystals. The flowers of this species are also reminiscent of the flower heads of composite plants; they are stalkless, up to 3.5 cm in diameter, golden-yellow and bloom in South Africa's semideserts from August till November. The fruit is a capsule that often opens only after it has been moistened.

67

Most of the extraordinary members of this genus were discovered during the first half of the 20th century, a time which brought descriptions of hundreds of new species, descriptions that included not only morphological but also ecological data. It was this information that was important for increasing the numbers of these succulents in cultivation. Their relatively modest requirements have made them great favourites with growers and collectors.

Schwantesia pillansii L. Bol. (69) is a South African succulent with upright to spreading leaves which are keeled, pointed, entire, glabrous, and coloured blue-green, often marbled on the surface, with reddish edges. They are 5 cm long and barely 5 mm wide.

Argyroderma carinatum L. Bol. (70) is a stemless succulent with short decussate leaves. They are ovate in outline with a whitish, unspotted surface. The short-stalked flowers adorn the semiarid stony slopes of Cape Province.

68

69

70

71

Echeveria minor (Rose) Bgr. (71) is a small succulent found in the semideserts of California. The leaves, tinged blue-green, are fleshy, shortly pointed, up to 5 cm long, 1 to 3 cm wide, and usually arranged in rosettes so that they resemble Europe's houseleeks (sempervivums). The terminal inflorescence, up to 25 cm long, is borne at the top of the leafy, purplish stem rising from the dense basal rosette. A characteristic feature of this species is the great variability of the leaves and flowers, which range in colour from yellow to purple.

Dorotheanthus bellidiformis (Burm. fil.) N. E. Br. (72) is a strikingly coloured species from Cape Province where it forms carpets of large, brightly coloured, daisylike flowers in the semiarid environment. They occur in a variety of hues, ranging from white, through pale pink to purplish-red, and have red anthers. The leaves are fleshy, ovate in outline, about 7 cm long and 10 mm wide, rough and warty. The stems are characterized by irregular thickening, caused by special tissue, in the form of 'annual rings'.

Frithia pulchra N. E. Br. (73) is another South African succulent that grows in the mountain districts of Transvaal. It is stemless and forms a rosette of erect, conical to cylindrical leaves about 2 cm long, with a flat tip and a rough surface covered with translucent dots. The flowers are solitary, sessile or short-stalked, about 2.5 cm in diameter, and coloured carmine-red with a white centre or else gleaming white. The flowers open fully in the heat of the midday sun. The plants are sporadically distributed throughout the seemingly inhospitable, stony terrain.

Lithops karasmontana (Dtr. et Schwant.) N. E. Br. (74) is found in the stony soil of Namibia in southwest Africa. It is a miniature succulent noted for its attractive large flowers with linear petals. The stem is only 3 to 4 cm high, pearly grey with a brown-spotted top. The picture shows the variety *summitatum* (Dtr.) de Boer et Boom, characterized by the reddish-brown network pattern on the top.

Lithops villetii L. Bol. (75) has a longish-ovoid stem, a little over 3 cm high, that branches near the top. The flowers, about 3 cm across, grow singly from the wide groove on top of the stem.

72

Lithops lesliei (N. E. Br.) Schwant. (76) is a miniature succulent native to Cape Province, Orange Free State and southwest Africa (Namibia). The small stem is broadly needle-like with a domed top covered with translucent dots. This part of the stem serves the same purpose as the 'windows' in the genus *Fenestraria* (Fig. 67). The plant is barely 4 cm high and about 3 cm wide. The flowers are solitary and grow from the groove on top.

Euphorbia grandicornis Goebel (77) is a spiny succulent spurge found in the tropical regions of Tanzania and Kenya, extending from this east African tableland to Natal in South Africa. The stem is upright, thick and fleshy, broadly winged, and branching in tiers. The entire surface is covered with rigid spines up to 5 cm long arranged in star-like formations. The individual flowers with jointed stalks are arranged in short-stalked cymose inflorescences. The schizocarpic fruit splits into separate, coral-red sections arranged round a central columella from which they shoot out in all directions with a loud popping sound.

73

74

75

76

Euphorbia milii des Martins (78) is a lovely and very attractive tufted spurge of a xerophilous nature. In its native Madagascar it is extremely variable, chiefly in the arrangement and colour of the cymose inflorescences. The leaves are longish-ovate, entire and blunt. The spines are up to 1 cm long and about 2 mm thick, and serve to protect mainly the lovely, blood-red flowers from being nibbled by animals. This Madagascar species is a popular ornamental plant not only in the greenhouse but also for room decoration.

Euphorbia horrida Boiss (79) looks like a cactus. It is native to Cape Province, where its stems, up to 15 cm thick, reach a height of 1 metre. They are deeply grooved and have 12 to 14 prominent longitudinal ribs. The inflorescences are stalked and emerge on the edges of the stems. This plant is noteworthy in that it is often host to the parasitic mistletoe *Viscum minimum.*

Carruanthus peersii L. Bol. (80) has a short stem rising from a leaf rosette. The leaves are upright with spiny-toothed margins, about 5 cm long, 10 to 15 mm wide and conspicuously triangular in cross section. The large flowers, up to 4 cm in diameter, are always yellow, but sometimes the tips of the petals are tinged pink. This species belongs to the family Mesembryan-themaceae, noted for the great variability of its flowers, which unlike

77

78

85

79

80

86

members of the cactus family have few perianth segments arranged in a ring. The two families have similar morphological characters produced by the long-term influence of similar or even identical environments. This condition is called convergence. Though plants living a long time in a similar environment resemble each other at first glance they are not related, or at most very distantly, and detailed examination of the seemingly similar organs reveals marked differences.

Crassula marnieriana Huber et Jacobs (81) is a succulent perennial from the tropical regions of eastern Africa. The long cylindrical stem is thickly covered with sessile leaves, broadly cordate-orbicular in outline (about 4 cm long and 8 mm wide), glabrous and bluish-pruinose with reddish edges. The flowers, arranged in dense terminal cymes or cymose panicles, are tiny and faintly bell-shaped. The generic name of this plant is derived from the Latin word *crassus,* meaning thick.

81

Chapter 3   CARNIVOROUS PLANTS

Carnivorous plants include members of various families related only very distantly. They include certain peculiar species of green plants which live in nitrogen deficient situations, for instance peat bogs, in both the temperate and tropical regions of the world. Though the plants contain chlorophyll and normally carry on photosynthesis, they cannot obtain enough nitrogen from the soil to maintain full vigour and seed production. Various adaptations, usually of the leaves, enable the plants to trap small insects and nitrogenous substances and perhaps mineral salts are absorbed from the insect bodies after they have been decomposed or digested.

Sundews (genus *Drosera*) live in temperate regions and they have leaves, covered with glandular trichomes, that secrete a sticky fluid containing an enzyme which digests the small insects that alight on the leaf surface.

The leaves of the tropical, epiphytic pitcher plants *(Nepenthes)* are modified into lidded pitcher-like organs which contain a secretion that digests the proteins of insect bodies. The inside walls of the pitcher are extremely smooth and slippery and covered with glandular, downward-growing hairs. Insects crawling on the surface of the pitcher slide down the smooth edge of the inside wall into the liquid at the bottom in which they drown and are gradually digested.

Leaf movements are sometimes quite extraordinary when it comes to trapping insects. In general they are responses to chemical stimuli. The Venus's Flytrap *(Dionaea muscipula)*, for instance, traps insects within its leaves by snapping shut the two halves along the midrib and joining the fringed margins. Butterworts (genus *Pinguicula*) curl the entire leaf margin, whereas bladderworts (genus *Utricularia*) have leaves modified into small bladders that suck in water with the aid of the hairs round the opening; this is fitted with a special lid that opens only inward thereby preventing the insects and crustaceans trapped inside from escaping. The unusual characteristics of the above plants indicate the widely varied paths taken by the evolutionary development of plant life and simultaneously how their manner of feeding has become diversified. Many species of carnivorous plants are extremely rare members of the flora of the respective regions where they occur and in some parts of the world their existence is already gravely endangered.

83

84

85

90

Venus's Flytrap (82) is found in the southeastern parts of North America. The leaves are
Dionaea muscipula   composed of two parts, a leaf-like glandless stalk and a rounded two-
Ell.   lobed blade with stiff nonsensory bristles on the margin. The upper
surface is covered with minute glands which secrete proteolytic enzymes and it bears three stiff bristles which when touched or irritated
cause the leaf lobes to snap shut with lightning speed thus trapping the
insect. Though they close in less than a second the lobes do not open
again until six days later to release the remnants of the devoured victim.
The Venus's Flytrap is the first instance of an insectivorous species to
be discovered in the plant realm — it was found in the swamplands of
North Carolina in 1760 by Governor A. Dobbs, who devoted much
time to its observation.

Common Sundew (83—84) is a perennial plant found in wet, peaty meadows from lowland to
Drosera rotundifolia   foothill districts. The long-stalked, basal leaves, either slightly raised or
L.   pressed to the ground, are arranged in a ground rosette. The leaf blades
are orbicular and covered on the upper side with long, red, glandular
hairs that secrete drops of sticky fluid. It is these glandular hairs that
serve to capture insects. The tiny white flowers are arranged in a loose
spike at the top of the leafless stems that rise from the centre of the
leaf rosette. Characteristic of this plant, which is distributed throughout
practically all Europe, is its great partiality to damp conditions. That is
why it is often found amidst sphagnum, which retains water for a long
time.

86

87   88

Cape Province Sundew (85), as its name indicates, is native to Cape Province. It has elongate
Drosera capensis L. leaves curled in a spiral at first. They, too, are covered with sensitive glandular hairs capable of digesting a great many small insects. The terminal racemose inflorescence is composed of 5 to 20 purplish-red flowers. The plant roots, usually thick and coloured black, soon die back, their function being taken over by adventitious roots.

    The genus *Drosera* numbers some 95 species distributed chiefly in the southern hemisphere — in Brazil, southern and tropical Africa, Australia and southeastern Asia; only a few, less striking species are found in the temperate regions of the northern hemisphere.

Pitcher Plant (86) is a hybrid developed by crossing *N. northiana* Hook. fil. and *N. maxima*
Nepenthes × *mixta* Reinw. Both parents are distributed in the tropics in the Indo-Malayan
Mast. archipelago to New Guinea where they grow as epiphytes. The leaves are flat with the midrib extended into a tendril terminated by a lidded pitcher for trapping insects. The inner walls of the pitchers are covered with digestive glands that produce enzymes which digest the bodies of trapped insects to provide the plant with the nitrogenous substances lacking in its diet. The hybrid has pitchers up to 30 cm long, coloured yellow-green spotted red at the bottom and with chestnut-brown spots on the rim. The genus *Nepenthes* includes some 70 species found mostly in southeast Asia and very occasionally in Madagascar and Sri Lanka.

Bladderwort (87) is an aquatic plant with submerged stems and leaves. Only the flower-bearing
Utricularia australis stem, terminated by a scanty racemose inflorescence, rises above the
R. Br. (syn. *U.* water. The leaves are divided into green, thread-like segments, some of
neglecta Lehm.) which are modified into hollow inflated bladders. The large bilabiate
flowers are striking with a long upper lip and a flat lower lip with an
undulate margin. This species is found in still waters throughout all
temperate Europe excepting the northern parts; also in South Africa
and Australia. Other species of aquatic bladderworts have two types of
leaves: green, thread-like leaves without bladders and non-green reduced leaf segments with bladders.

Butterwort (88) is an important Mexican species characterized by a basal leaf rosette composed
Pinguicula gypsicola of elongate leaves widened broadly at the base and curved upward at
Brandeg. the tip. The upper surface is thickly covered with stalked glands secret-
ing a sticky fluid. Amidst these are sessile glands containing digestive
enzymes. The first type serves to trap small insects, then the enzymes
digest their bodies into substances which can be absorbed by the plant.
The flowers are solitary, large (up to 5 cm across), purple and borne on
long stems thickly covered with glands.

Butterwort (89) is a rare Mexican species from Oaxaca Province where it grows at high moun-
Pinguicula tain elevations up to 2,500 metres above sea level. The bottom leaves
rotundifolia are arranged in a rosette and are spoon-shaped at the tip, whereas the
Studnička upper leaves are longish-ovate, ciliate on the upper surface and conspicuously glandular. The colour of the single, terminal flower is
extremely variable.

89

90

91

Butterwort (90) is a perennial species found in the muddy mountain meadows of Mexico and *Pinguicula lilacina* Schlecht. et Cham. Guatemala. The flowering stem with a single striking blossom grows from a simple rhizome. The leaves, arranged in a ground rosette, are fleshy, broadly ovate, 2 to 4 cm long and covered with tiny narrow glands on the upper surface.

Butterwort (91) is found on damp mossy rocks or near mountain brooks in Mexico. The leaves *Pinguicula caudata* Schlecht. are broadly ovate, the flower stalks may grow up to 15 cm in length. Since this species varies greatly in the colour of its flowers, there is considerable confusion with regard to its status within the genus.

Byblis liniflora Salisb. (92) derives its name from the Greek word *byblos,* meaning paper, perhaps because the narrow, yellow-green leaves, up to 20 cm long and furled like a cornucopia, are very fine and paper thin. The minute glands resemble those of the insectivorous sundews (see species nos. 83—85). The glands on the linear leaves are either stalked or sessile and arranged in rows according to the distribution of the epidermal cells. The flowers are solitary, 5-merous and long-stalked. The genus *Byblis* includes only two species, both of which are found only in northern and western Australia and represents a very isolated group of plants.

92

Chapter 4   ORCHIDS

The graceful flowers of orchids, resembling an irregular lily in appearance, are of all kinds of lovely shapes and colours. Borne in racemose inflorescences they have six perianth segments arranged in an outer and inner whorl with the lowest perianth segment of the inner whorl differing in shape, size and colour from the others. This segment is called the lip and in some species is extended into a spur, often many times longer than the flower itself. In the bud the lip is located at the top but because the flower is spirally twisted a full 180° as it opens it becomes the basal segment.

The requirements of orchids, some 90 percent of which are distributed in tropical Asia, Africa and South America, depend on the manner in which they obtain food. The tropical rain forests with their abundant rainfall and high atmospheric moisture provide an excellent environment for the epiphytic species which absorb water through their aerial roots. Their long stems, reaching for the light by climbing up to the treetops, are jointed and the segments are usually modified into pseudobulbs that serve as storage organs. In terrestrial species, which have much shorter stems, food stores for the growth and development of further generations are located in underground root tubers.

The roots of some species of orchids are inhabited by special mycorrhizal fungi which provide the orchid with water containing dissolved minerals from the surrounding environment. In species containing chlorophyll such mycorrhizas serve merely to supplement the plants' diet but in the case of orchids that have no green colouring matter they are the plants' sole means of obtaining food.

Orchids are a relatively young group from an evolutionary aspect. It is believed that about 50 to 60 million years ago their terrestrial ancestors were confined to southeast Asia, including present-day Indonesia. The change to an epiphytic way of life probably took place only about 5 million years ago. Fossil orchids (imprints) are barely 2 million years old and are relatively rare. In the present day orchids are without doubt passing through a period of intensive evolution as

94

95

reflected by the appearance of a great many interspecific as well as intergeneric hybrids in nature. If to this we add the hybrids developed in cultivation the final count is nearly 25,000 different kinds of orchids. Though this chapter presents only a small fraction, those depicted have been selected to demonstrate the immense diversity of this group of plants.

Butterfly Orchid (93) text see page 113

Cattleya mossiae Parker (94) is an epiphytic orchid of the tropical rain forests of Venezuela where it blooms in May and June. It is extremely variable, particularly in the shape of the flower and colour of the lip, and that is the reason for the many described varieties. It has fleshy, conical pseudobulbs up to 20 cm long bearing two leathery leaves up to 25 cm long and 8 cm wide. The flower stalk, growing from the axil of the leaf-sheath at the base of each leaf, is terminated by a raceme of two to five huge flowers measuring up to 18 cm across! Both the outer and inner segments are finely crenate on the margins; the outer segments are elliptic, the inner ones broadly elliptic, and the middle lobe of the striking three-lobed lip is a different colour.

Cattleya × hybrida hort. (95) is an example of an interspecific hybrid developed in cultivation. The specific name clearly indicates its hybrid origin and the abbreviation hort. serves to explain that the hybridization took place in greenhouse cultivation. The aim of such hybridization under controlled temperature, light and soil conditions, including soil and atmospheric moisture, is to develop plants with large, attractively coloured and long-lasting flowers. It is often very difficult to designate the parent species from which a hybrid takes its origin because in extensive cultivation there are always instances of the spontaneous development of interspecific hybrids that gradually become increasingly remote from the original parent species. Though it is possible to make a guess as to the probable origin of such a hybrid by comparing the perianths, the prevailing colour or the markings on the perianth segments, the value of a cultivated orchid is determined not by taxonomic origin but by other criteria — namely general appearance and colouration. The name given to the hybrid generally expresses these traits, for instance *Cattleya × Fabia alba* hort., etc.

Cattleya intermedia Grah. (96) is a species with relatively large blossoms up to 15 cm across, arranged in two- to seven-flowered racemes. The outer segments are broadly elliptic, sometimes with a pointed tip, the inner segments much wider with the tip and the margin slightly undulating or revolute. This

96

97

orchid is an epiphyte and therefore has thickened, cylindrical pseudo-bulbs up to 25 cm long usually terminated by a single large leaf coloured fresh green. It is native to the rain forests of Brazil where it produces flowers in the autumn months.

Phalaenopsis esmeralda Rchb. f. (97) is an epiphyte of the tropical forests of southeast Asia (syn. *Doritis* and is distributed throughout a vast range extending from Burma *pulcherrima* Ldl.) through Thailand and Laos to Sumatra, where it flowers in autumn. The blossoms are relatively small and arranged in thick, upright, slightly branched racemes composed of 15 to 20 flowers. They vary in colour from pale pink to dark purple with the lip always differing slightly in colour from the other segments.

Phalaenopsis amabilis (L.) Bl. (98) grows as an epiphyte on tropical trees and shrubs in Indonesia and New Guinea and bears flowers over a very long period — from October to March. It does not have pseudobulbs. The flower stalks that grow from the axils of the short leaf-sheaths at the base of the fleshy leaves are terminated by slender, racemose inflorescences composed of six to twenty shapely flowers. The outer perianth segments are elliptic with a prominent keel, the inner segments are of similar shape but slightly recurved. The lip is deeply three-lobed with upright side lobes and the middle lobe is prolonged into two hair-like outgrowths.

98

Phalaenopsis × hybrida hort. (99) is an interspecific hybrid obtained by crossings in cultivation. According to the structure and colour of the flowers *P. amabilis* (L.) Bl. and *P. schilleriana* Rchb. f. are the species from which it was most probably derived. The first is native to Indonesia and New Guinea (see species no. 98), the second is from the Philippines. The genus *Phalaenopsis* numbers some 70 species which grow on tree trunks or even the damp walls of abandoned structures in the tropical regions of northeastern India, all of southeastern Asia, Indonesia, the Philippines and northern Australia, where they form numerous interspecific hybrids. Like cattleyas these orchids are valued for their aesthetic qualities by both growers and the general public. Inasmuch as the members of this genus grow in the damp lowland tropics of Asia their chief requirements in greenhouse cultivation are ample heat and atmospheric moisture. It is a known fact that rapid growth is promoted in particular by flowing air.

99

100

× **Brassocattleya hybrida** hort. (100) is an intergeneric hybrid obtained by crossings in cultivation with probably *Brassavola flagellaris* Rodr. and *Cattleya bicolor*
Ldl. figuring in its parentage. Each of the two species has distinctive
characters which combined in hybridization produce striking effects,
chiefly in the shape of the flower and the pink and white colouration of
the lip. Intergeneric crossings may involve even three genera, for instance *Brassavola, Laelia* and *Cattleya,* in which case the resulting hybrid is designated as × *Brassolaeliocattleya hybrida.* The combination
of a greater number of characters has endowed such hybrids, obtained
by crossings between two and three genera, with properties chiefly in
the shape and colour of the blossoms, that could never have been
developed spontaneously in nature, where the respective genera (used
in the crossings) do not occur together in the same locality.

101

Aerides odoratum Lour. (101) has a stem, up to 1 metre high, covered with strap-shaped, yellow-green leaves up to 25 cm long and broadly sheathed at the base. The dense, stalked inflorescences grow from the leaf axils. This species is epiphytic and is found on tropical trees and shrubs in the rain forests of India and southeast Asia, its range extending to southern China, Indonesia and the Philippines. It usually flowers from July till November.

Paphiopedilum sukhakulii Sengh. et Schos. (102) is a terrestrial species of Thailand's jungle forests where it occurs up to elevations of 1,000 metres. It was discovered there only recently, in 1964, by the well-known Thai orchid collector Sukhakul. It has a root tuber which bears a rosette of elliptic leaves up to 25 cm long and 4 to 5 cm wide, marbled pale green above and dotted with red beneath. Like all members of this genus this orchid is noted for its inflated, pouch-like lip enclosing the column called the gynostemium, consisting of the united stamens and style. The flower stalk is up to 25 cm long and terminated by a single flower (very occasionally two) up to 12 cm across with expanding segments above the lip that are up to 6 cm long and wavy on the margin.

104

Paphiopedilum × **maudiae** hort. (103) is a hybrid obtained in cultivation by crossings between *P. lawrenceanum* Pfitz. and *P. callosum* (Rchb. f.) Pfitz. The first of the parent species is native to Borneo and the second is an important species of tropical Thailand. From the geographic distribution of the two it is evident that spontaneous hybridization in the wild is out of the question for their ranges are entirely separate. The illustrated hybrid has a strikingly coloured pouch, deep purplish-brown with a pale green edge; the other segments are yellowish-white with purple veins at the tip and dark green longitudinal veins at the base.

102

103   104

Paphiopedilum × **mouquetieanum** Pfitz. (104) is a natural hybrid between two Sumatran species — *P. rothschildianum* Pfitz. and *P. chamberlainianum* Pfitz. Both parents flower in the autumn and are found in the tropical mountain forests of Sumatra at elevations of approximately 2,000 metres. The blossoms of the hybrid are up to 10 cm across. The outer segments are greenish-white with dark veins and a lobed margin covered with minute glands, the inner segments are expanded and coloured greenish with purplish-red spots. The lip is green, finely spotted with purple inside. A noteworthy characteristic of all hybrids of this genus is the extraordinary longevity of the blossoms which last for several weeks.

Paphiopedilum insigne (Wall. ex Ldl.) Pfitz. (105) is a terrestrial orchid found in tropical Assam in northeastern India at elevations of 1,000 to 2,000 metres. It is a rare species in its native land and flowers from September to December. The leaves are strap-shaped, up to 25 cm long and barely 3 cm wide, dark green on the upper surface and spotted with violet on the underside at the base. The flower stalk, coloured dark purple, is up to 30 cm high and terminated by a single flower (very occasionally two) 7 cm across. The outer segments are yellow-green with white tips and prominent reddish-brown veins, the inner segments are blunt, expanded, yellow to yellow-green with dark purple spots along the veins. The lip is yellow-green finely dotted with brownish violet inside the pouch.

Paphiopedilum glaucophyllum J.J.Sm. (106) is a beautifully coloured terrestrial orchid growing in the tropical forests of Java. The leaves have blunt tips and have a bluish-green tinge. The long flower stalk is terminated by a single flower, measuring up to 10 cm across, with whitish-yellow outer segments striped dark green at the base, long lateral inner segments coloured yellowish-green with red spots and a downy margin, and a dingy violet pouch. The diverse shapes and spatial arrangements of the individual segments give the strikingly large blossom a superb symmetry. The genus *Paphiopedilum* is distinguished by two important characteristics: the lower petal is converted to a striking, inflated, moccasin-shaped pouch and the geographical distribution is confined to southeast Asia, including northeastern India, neighbouring Indonesia and the Philippines.

105

106

107

× **Laeliocattleya hybrida** hort. (107) is an example of an intergeneric hybrid (a cross between the genera *Laelia* and *Cattleya*) which differs from the parent plants chiefly by its phenological characteristics (it flowers twice a year), and by having flowers that are larger and of slightly different shape. It is well known that members of the genus *Cattleya* readily interbreed with members of other genera, usually species of *Laelia* and *Brassavola*.

Zygopetalum mackaii Hook. (108) is a very attractive epiphytic orchid of the rain forests of Brazil, where it flowers from November to February, its extraordinarily large clusters offer a particularly striking sight against the uniform green of the tropical vegetation. The pseudobulbs climbing up the tree trunks bear leaves that are longish-elliptic in outline (up to 40 cm long and barely 3 cm wide) and prominently veined. Rising from the leaf axils are racemose inflorescences composed of five to ten flowers and reaching a length of more than 90 cm. The individual flowers, borne along one side of the long, horizontal axis, are up to 7 cm across and have a characteristically shaped lip with small side lobes and a flat, slightly curved middle lobe.

108

Brassavola perrinii Ldl. (109) is an epiphytic orchid growing in the tropical forests of Brazil where it flowers in May and June. It has very slender pseudobulbs measuring up to 20 cm in length and bearing linear, grooved leaves. The flowers, arranged in clusters of three to eight, measure 7 cm across. Fully opened blossoms may last up to a month. In cultivation members of this genus readily interbreed with members of the genus *Cattleya* (see species no. 100); the intergeneric hybrids are noted for their beautifully coloured lips.

Lady of the Night (110) is a pretty, small, epiphytic orchid growing from slender pseudobulbs
Brassavola nodosa to a length of about 15 cm, with narrow, fleshy, grooved leaves twice
(L.) Ldl. the length of the stem. The racemose inflorescence, often up to 20 cm

109

110

110

long, is composed of six flowers at the most. These are of a remarkable size — up to 9 cm in length. All the segments, excepting the lip, are narrowly linear, whitish-green or yellowish and conspicuously flared. The striking lip is broadly heart-shaped, curved like a sickle when viewed from the side, and gleaming white with pale yellow veins and several tiny purple dots. This is a tropical and subtropical species distributed from Mexico through the Caribbean islands, Venezuela and Ecuador to Peru where it often bears flowers the whole year, though generally in autumn.

111

Gold Net Orchid (111, 112) is an epiphytic orchid native to the forests of Java, where it was *Macodes petola* Bl. discovered (by the Belgian botanist E. P. Dossin) at the turn of the 18th century. It is an unusual orchid in that it is noted not for its blossoms but for its spectacular foliage, which is dark green with a delicate network of golden-yellow veins, whence it derives the name Gold Net Orchid. The principal parallel veins are linked by branched, transverse veins so that the general effect is of a network with smaller and larger spaces. The leaves are broadly ovate, 5 to 7 cm long, usually 5 cm wide and short-stalked. From the axils of the leaf sheaths grow scanty racemes composed of several tiny pale brown flowers. Members of the genus *Macodes* are native to Java and New Guinea where they grow up to elevations of approximately 1,000 metres. They are variable particularly in size, leaf shape and colour of the veins. *M. petola* Bl. occurs as two varieties: var. *argenteireticulata* J. J. Sm. with silvery veins and var. *robusta* J. J. Sm., with large velvety leaves and golden-yellow veins. No other genus of orchids has such striking, prominently veined leaves.

Butterfly Orchid (93), an epiphytic species, has flat, oval pseudobulbs up to 5 cm high with *Oncidium papilio* leathery leaves that are longish-elliptic, pointed and covered with conspicuous brownish-red blotches. The flowers are arranged in striking, Ldl. loose racemes up to 1.5 metres long. Each flower resembles a butterfly

112

113

in flight, a fact reflected in the specific name *papilio,* meaning butterfly. The outer segments are up to 12 cm long, curved at the tip and rolled into a tube, whereas the inner segments, likewise curving in an arch, are flat and longish-elliptic. The lip has a large blotch in the centre and a broad, wavy margin. This species is distributed from Trinidad through Venezuela to Peru.

Oncidium guibertianum A. Rich. (113) is found in Cuba and certain other Caribbean islands. It is characterized by pendulous flower clusters up to 2 metres long, branching near the top and composed of relatively small flowers (4 cm in diameter) of variable colour; the lip is yellowish-white spotted with red at the base. All members of this genus are giant orchids noted chiefly for their robust stems and leaves.

Pleione limprichtii Schltr. (114) is an epiphytic mountain orchid found in the foothills of the central and eastern Himalayas at elevations of 1,000 to 2,500 metres, where it flowers in the autumn months (October to November). It has small pseudobulbs with leaves up to 20 cm long from the axils of which grow flower stalks bearing solitary flowers. These measure 6 to 8 cm in diameter and have a striking horn-shaped lip coloured golden-

114

yellow, often spotted with violet inside and finely fringed on the margin. The colouration of the flower is extremely variable. When fully open the flower droops like a bell.

Tiger Orchid (115) is
*Odontoglossum
grande* Ldl.
an important epiphytic orchid of the submontane tropical forests of southern Mexico and Guatemala where it grows up to elevations of 2,500 metres and flowers from October to March. The scientific name of this orchid aptly describes its characteristics — the generic name *Odontoglossum* refers to the shape of the flowers which resemble long tongues and the specific name *grande* refers to their large size, up to 15 cm across. All the members of this genus (some 100 species) are mountain orchids of tropical Central and South America and their occurrence at elevations of up to 3,000 metres is not at all unusual.

O. *grande* has racemose clusters up to 30 cm long composed of three to eight long-stalked flowers. The outer segments are longish-lanceolate and coloured yellow with large brownish-red blotches, the inner segments are wider and coloured brownish-red with yellowish tips. The lip is broadly ovate and creamy-white with brownish-red blotches at the base.

115

116

Lady's Slipper, Slipper Orchid (116, 117) with blossoms measuring up to 10 cm across is one of
Cypripedium
calceolus L.
the largest-flowered orchids of the temperate regions of Europe and
Asia. However, it is also found on the Atlantic coast of North America.
It grows in shaded broad-leaved woods, particularly on limestone substrates, from lowland to mountain elevations. The stem grows from
a creeping rhizome and bears three to five broadly elliptic, prominently
veined leaves clasping the stem. The flower stalk is terminated by
a single flower, though very occasionally there may be two, three or
even four. Most striking is the inflated pouch-like lip. The other perianth segments are arranged one above the lip (this is broad and upright
and composed of the two joined lateral segments of the outer whorl),
one below the lip (this is the third outer segment), and two (the remain-

ing inner segments) spreading on either side of the lip. This orchid is unfortunately endangered in the wild for, being relatively easy to grow, it is often dug up by those who wish to grow it in their garden.

Vanda coerulea Griff. ex Ldl. (118) is a distinctive epiphyte found in the east Himalayan foothills in India, Burma and Thailand. Its rigid stems climbing the trunks of tropical trees are about one metre long with long aerial roots that absorb atmospheric moisture. The leaves thickly covering the stem are leathery with irregularly toothed tips and are arranged in pairs

117

118

opposite one another. The flower clusters growing from the leaf axils are up to 50 cm long and are composed of 5 to 15 flowers. The flowering period is from September to December. A typical characteristic of this species is the great variability in the size and colour of the flowers, so that one plant may have pale blue, pale blue-violet as well as deep violet flowers in a single cluster. The lip is always small and three-lobed with the middle lobe conspicuously darker than the other parts of the flower.

The genus *Vanda* includes some 70 species distributed in the tropical and subtropical regions of Asia.

Dactylorhiza maculata (L.) Soó (119) is a terrestrial orchid of the temperate regions of Europe, (syn. *Orchis maculata* L.) Asia and North America where it grows chiefly in wet pastureland, peat meadows and heaths as well as in open woodlands and scrub from foothill to mountain districts. It forms underground root tubers

119

119

which bear long, upright stems terminated by a conical spike composed of a great many pale-violet to pinkish-white flowers.

Broad-leaved or Fen Orchid (120) is widely distributed in central Europe in damp or boggy
Dactylorhiza majalis meadows from lowland to mountain districts. It differs from the
(Rchb.) Hunt et preceding species by having a thickly leaved stem with the uppermost
Summerh. (syn. leaf reaching as far as the conical inflorescence which has reddish
Orchis latifolia L.) bracts longer than the flowers.

120

Phragmopedilum sedenii Pfitz. (121) is an evergreen terrestrial orchid native to the mountain forests of Ecuador and Peru where it is often encountered even at elevations of about 2,500 metres. It has longish elliptic leaves (up to 60 cm long) that are twisted like cornucopias and from whose axils grow robust stems up to 1 metre high topped by a single flower. An important character of identification, in addition to the slipper-like lip, are the extraordinarily long inner segments which reach a length of 25 cm and hang from the flower like twisted straps. The outer as well as the inner segments are a lighter colour than the dark lip, and the flower often has longitudinal stripes.

120

121   122

All species of the genus *Phragmopedilum* have a pouch-like lip, as do members of the genus *Paphiopedilum* (species nos. 102—106). They are popular orchids for greenhouse cultivation for the blossoms last a long time.

Dendrobium chrysotoxum Ldl. (122) is found in the tropics of northeastern India below the Himalayas, also in southern China, Laos and Thailand, from lowland districts to submontane forests. Like all other members of this large genus distributed in southeastern Asia and Australia it is an epiphyte. The illustrated species has large, conical pseudobulbs (up to 30 cm long), each bearing two to four leathery leaves. The pendulous raceme, nearly 25 cm long, is composed of 8 to 15 fragrant, golden-yellow flowers up to 4 cm across. The outer and inner segments are the same shape, broadly ovate and pointed. The lip is golden-yellow to orange-yellow (this is reflected in the Latin name of the species) and finely fringed.

Cymbidium × **hybridum** hort. (123) is a hybrid obtained in cultivation. Here, too, it is impossible to state with certainty the species from which it is derived for cymbidiums cross so readily and in such great numbers that a hybrid's parentage may include several species. Interbreeding is not so common in the wild where their epiphytic way of life makes mutual contact between species difficult, but in cultivation they are grown as ground orchids so that crossings between species are relatively easy. The range of distribution of the genus *Cymbidium* is very large, extending from the north Indian region below the Himalayas through southeastern Asia, southern China, Indonesia to Australia. The extreme variability in the colour and shape of the relatively large blossoms (particularly in hybrids) makes these orchids very popular with growers.

123

Angraecum eburneum Bory (124) takes its scientific name from the common Malayan name *angrec,* denoting that this is a climbing or epiphytic orchid. This species is found only in Madagascar where it flowers from November to January. The leaves are up to 50 cm long, pale green, and irregularly divided at the tip. The flowers are short-stalked, up to 6 cm across, and arranged in two rows. The outer and inner segments are both pale green, long-pointed and spreading; the lip, flat and narrowing into a long point, is pure white; the spur is slightly curved, pale green and up to 10 cm long.

124

125

Cirrhopetalum Ldl. (125) is an extroardinary genus of orchids with strikingly shaped flowers. The scientific name is derived from the Latin word *cirrhus,* meaning curl, and the Greek word *petalon,* meaning petal, a reference to the curled outer lateral segments which are a characteristic feature of this genus. The inner segments are small and the lip is also very small but movable, which serves to attract insect pollinators, chiefly dipterous insects. Members of the genus *Cirrhopetalum* are epiphytic plants found in the tropics of east Africa and Madagascar as well as in all of tropical Asia from northeastern India through southeast Asia, Indonesia to New Guinea. They include some 50 species that generally flower in the autumn and winter months.

126

Cirrhopetalum medusae Ldl. (126) is a very striking epiphytic orchid of the tropical forests of Malaysia, Sumatra and Borneo. The leaves growing from the pseudobulbs are leathery, strap-shaped, up to 20 cm long and coloured pale green. The flowers, clustered in dense capitate racemes in the axils of the leaf sheaths, resemble the head of a medusa with their long, hair-like outer segments and short inner segments.

Lycaste deppei Ldl. (127) is an epiphytic orchid of the tropical mountain forests of Guatemala and Mexico. The ovate pseudobulbs are up to 10 cm long. The strap-shaped leaves are up to 50 cm long, 10 cm wide and they are usually pointed at the tip. The erect, racemose inflorescences, which grow from the axils of the leaf sheaths, are only 15 cm long and composed of extremely fragrant and very long-lasting flowers. These have relatively long stalks and measure 8 to 10 cm across. The outer perianth segments are broadly elliptic and approximately 6 cm long, the inner segments are shorter and spread out on either side of the lip which is three-lobed. The genus *Lycaste* numbers some 35 species and has a wide distribution between Mexico and Brazil. It occurs at higher elevations between 1,500 and 2,500 metres in areas where there is a high rainfall. Most have lemon-yellow blossoms with a characteristic spicy fragrance, particularly penetrating at night. All members of this species are typical elements of the vegetation of tropical mist forests where a high atmospheric moisture content is maintained both during the daytime and at night.

127

Catasetum fimbriatum Ldl. (128) has strikingly large, racemose inflorescences up to 40 cm long and composed of 7 to 15 flowers. The perianth segments, relatively small, elongate and pointed, are yellowish with dark red spots. The horn-like lip is yellow with a prominently fringed margin. This orchid, native to Brazil, has two different kinds of flowers: the male flowers are slightly smaller and of a paler hue, the female flowers larger and darker. This condition is called dimorphism. In the tropical forests of Brazil the orchid grows as an epiphyte together with tens of other related species of the same genus, differing chiefly in the colour of the flowers.

Horned Orchid (129) differs somewhat from other orchids in the shape of the flower. The lip is
Stanhopea divided into three lobes and the other segments are all recurved. It is
hernandezi Schltr. an epiphyte found in the rain forests of Mexico, Ecuador and Peru from lowland to submontane elevations.

129

Chapter 5   AQUATIC, MARSHLAND AND SHORELINE PLANTS

Throughout the world bodies of water and expanses of inundated shoreline host numerous species of plants, which together with aquatic animals form unique biological communities. Their diversity corresponds to the character of these environments, ranging from shallow seas and coastal lagoons, to freshwater lakes, ponds and rivers and all their large and small tributaries where one will find all kinds of flowering plants (dicotyledons and monocotyledons). The composition of such communities around inland waters is far more diverse than in the seas and oceans because the shores of still and flowing waters may consist of vast marshy areas which provide exceptionally good conditions for the development of plant communities. Plants of flowing and still water or wet banks and shorelines are distributed throughout the whole world regardless of the climatic conditions. That is why they are found in the tropics as well as in temperate regions and at high latitudes in both the northern and southern hemispheres. The decisive factor for their growth and development is not the climate, temperature or rainfall, but the presence of a continuous expanse of water and the purity of the water. Fluctuations in the water level during the course of the year are an important factor affecting the anchorage and growth of aquatic and shoreline plants. In lakes, ponds and oxbow lakes decisive factors are the depth of the water, its temperature, clarity, the minerals it contains, and the presence of plankton and larger animals. Still waters provide congenial conditions for the growth of many species of shoreline plants. In the case of rivers and streams, on the other hand, the determining factor is the speed of the current, which is influenced by the depth, width and gradient of the bed as well as by the configuration of the surrounding landscape, for a river in the mountains is quite different from a river in a wide valley or in flat, spreading lowland country. Many plant species also maintain a foothold on rocks and boulders in rapids or waterfalls and so water provides a wide choice for the plants and animals that make this environment their home. The aquatic environment and its surroundings are affected by the natural aging of these habitats (for example the invasion of bodies of water by vegetation and the consequent silting up with soil). These phenomena pose no threat to plant communities. However the pollution of water by various

131

industrial wastes is an entirely different matter and this has an immeasurable effect on aquatic communities. If we wish to take continued delight in the beautifully coloured blossoms of aquatic plants and the deep green vegetation bordering watersides we must take care how we use this environment, for water courses are very vulnerable and readily damaged by pollution, be it occasional or constant, and the number of plant species that have paid dearly as a result of man's thoughtless actions is continually increasing.

White Water-lily (130) text see page 136

Victoria amazonica (Pöpp.) Sowerby (131) forms gigantic leaves, sometimes nearly 4 but usu-
(syn. *Vict* ally 2 metres across, which grow directly from an underwater rhizome,
Lindl.) in South America's tropical rivers. The raised, upcurved leaf margin is 6 to 10 cm high so that viewed from a distance it looks as if huge, shallow dishes were floating on the water — truly a fascinating sight! The upper surface of the leaves is pale green, the under surface purple with many veins arranged in a fan-like pattern that greatly reinforces and strengthens the leaves as long as they are in water. The fragrant flowers have thick spiny stalks that grow directly from the rhizomes; they are huge — about 30 to 40 cm in diameter — and nocturnal, opening

133

on two successive evenings, after which they develop underwater into a fleshy fruit with black seeds. The seeds are eaten by the native Indians who call them 'water maize'. The first European to see this plant was the Czech Tadeáš Haenke, who came across it in the Río Mamoré swamps in Bolivia in 1801 and the first to describe it in 1832 was the German traveller Pöppig; the English botanist J. Lindley later named it in honour of Queen Victoria. The natives call it *irupé*.

Victoria cruziana d'Orb. (132) is found in the Paraná River region between north Argentina and Paraguay. This plant astounded all those who travelled through South America, particularly botanists — all undertook difficult and dangerous journeys to get a glimpse of its magnificent flowers. The leaves of this plant are reinforced on the underside by rigid, reddish ribs, or leaf veins. The edges are raised 8 to 10 cm above the water thereby accentuating the size of the blade, which is a about 120 cm across. The flower bud is conical, pointed, yellowish-green and enclosed by a green spiny calyx at the base. The expanded flowers are white. The fruits develop underwater, splitting at maturity to release the seeds.

Branched Bur-reed (133) is characterized by its great adaptability to changing conditions in its
Sparganium erectum aquatic and shoreline environment. It is widespread in oxbow lakes and
L. em. Rchb. irrigation ditches but is also found in pond margins where it is generally part of the encroaching shoreline vegetation growing under swampy conditions in shallow water. The flowers are arranged in a panicle-like inflorescence composed of globose heads, 2 to 5 female heads at the bottom and 17 to 20 male heads at the top. The leaves, which grow from a stout, stoloniferous rhizome, are stiff, erect, three-angled at the base and keeled at the tip. They usually jut above the water but may also float on the surface.

Nymphaea zanzibariensis Caspary (134) is a perennial anchored by stout rhizomes in the mud of the tropical waters of Zanzibar and eastern Africa. The leaves are stiff, orbicular, 20 to 40 cm long, lobed on the margin and palmately veined on the undersurface. As in all floating aquatics the pores through which the plant breathes are located on the upper surface, with none on the underside which is not exposed to the air. The leaf

134

135

136

137

blades either float on the water or else rise above the water as the stalks lengthen. The leaf stalks, as well as the flower stalks, contain aerenchymatous tissue with large air-filled spaces between the cells; this sponge-like tissue serves to buoy up the plant organs. The attractive, solitary flowers are up to 25 cm in diameter and last about 5 days. They open in the daytime, about 15 cm above the water. Members of the genus *Nymphaea* are perennial aquatics unlike the tropical victorias (see species nos. 131 and 132) which are annuals.

White Water-lily (130, 135) has long-stalked leaves that float on the water or rise above the
Nymphaea alba L.   surface. They are leathery, broadly elliptical with a deep, wide basal cleft and they grow from thick, creeping rhizomes concealed in the muddy bottom. The flowers are composed of a great many petals coloured white, sometimes pink, and a large number of yellow stamens. The plant is typical of still waters of the temperate to subtropical regions of Eurasia.

136

Yellow Water-lily (136, 137) is found in still and slow-flowing water throughout the temperate
Nuphar lutea (L.) Sm. regions of Eurasia, where it forms an attractive colour contrast to
the delicate White Water-lily in whose company it grows. The flowers,
with yellow sepals enclosing the inner organs like a cup, last a long
time. The fleshy fruit is bottle-shaped and ripens underwater. The
broadly-ovate, leathery leaf blades float on the water or jut above the
surface.

Amphibious Bistort (138) is noted for its deep-pink spike-like inflorescences. It forms
Polygonum characteristic colonies on still and slow-flowing water. The large, elon-
amphibium L. gate leaves, coloured deep green, float on the surface. Out of water, for
instance in environments such as muddy fields, damp ditches, and mud-
dy pond margins, it occurs as a terrestrial form with erect stems, long-
stalked leaves which are downy on the margin, and with pinkish flowers clustered in a large, short raceme.

138

139

Flowering Rush (139) grows in shallow water or wet mud at the irregular and usually over-
Butomus umbellatus L. grown edges of still bodies of water or slow-flowing water courses.
The stem is terminated by an umbel-like inflorescence composed of
long-stalked flowers growing from the axils of scale-like bracts; their
pale pink colour is very pretty against the green of the shoreline vegetation. The flowering stem grows from a stout horizontal rhizome to
a height of 1.5 metres and is enclosed at the base by a rosette of linear
leaves. Each leaf is sheath-like and three-angled at the base but the
upper half is flattened. Flowering Rush is distributed throughout practically all of Europe and Asia excepting the Far East. It is a perennial
herb that roots readily from pieces of detached rhizome. The rhizomes

are carried great distances by the water, catching and rooting in deep layers of humus by the shoreline. Asexual reproduction by vegetative means — by pieces of roots, rhizomes, stems and leaves — is typical of aquatic and marshland plants.

Arrowhead (140, 141) derives its name from the Latin word *sagitta,* meaning arrow, a reference
Sagittaria sagittifolia L. to the shape of the leaves, many of which resemble an arrowhead. They are of very diverse shape. The submerged leaves are linear, the floating leaves elliptic or sagittate and the long-stalked aerial leaves sharply arrow-shaped. The inflorescence is erect and composed of short-stalked flowers arranged in whorls of three. The stamens and pistils are arranged in a spiral. Arrowhead grows in fresh and brackish water in temperate or tropical regions throughout the world. Species no. 140 is var. *sinensis* Whn. — a robust perennial herb up to 2 metres high that often covers pools and the backwaters of large water courses.

140

141

Marestail (142) is found in still or flowing water as well as in wet marshland where its simple,
Hippuris vulgaris L. thickly leaved stems grow straight upward to a height of 50 cm. The leaves, arranged in whorls of six to twelve, are linear and completely conceal the tiny axillary flowers which have fully aborted corollas. Large masses of Marestail look very much like masses of Horsetail, which often include the former. The species is distributed throughout all temperate and northern Eurasia eastward to Japan; it is also found in North America.

Water Hyacinth (143) is a typical plant of the still, shallow and warm waters of the subtropical
Eichhornia crassipes and tropical regions of America though it also forms large masses in
Solms tropical waters throughout the world. Its mass occurrence in dams is

unwelcome, however, for large colonies of this plant reduce the amount of oxygen in the water and thereby cause the death of large numbers of fish; the plants furthermore prevent the penetration of light to the deeper layers and thus retard the growth of other vegetation. The Water Hyacinth forms irregular rosettes of long-stalked, heart-shaped, pointed leaves on the surface. The leaf stalks are greatly swollen and float on the water. The flowers are large, fragrant and pale violet, and stagnant pools or backwaters covered with masses of these flowers resemble a colourful, constantly undulating carpet.

142

143

Purple Loosestrife (144) is commonly found in waterside thickets and damp meadows but most
Lythrum salicaria L.   of all at the wet, irregular shoreline of still or flowing water. Its tall,
erect stems, up to 2 metres high, are often seen on wide shorelines or
littoral zones. The leaves are sessile and bluish-violet with prominent
veins. The flowers, coloured red, are arranged at the tips of the stems in
branching racemes, blossoming in succession from the bottom upward.
This species is distributed throughout all Eurasia to the Arctic Circle
and eastward to Japan and has also become naturalized in eastern
North America and Australia.

Monkey Flower (145) is a very striking plant of wet, muddy situations or the moist edges of
Mimulus guttatus DC.   flowing water, often spreading alongside meadow brooks, chiefly in
piedmont districts. It is native to all of North America, where it extends
to Alaska and the Aleutian Islands. In South America it is found along
the Pacific coast, from Colombia to Chile, and in the Old World it is
naturalized in central and northern Europe, including Great Britain.
The leaves are opposite and undivided, those at the top of the stem
being heart-shaped with a toothed margin, and they are more thickly
covered with glands than the 75 cm high stem. The flowers, growing from the upper leaf axils, are large and trumpet-shaped with five,
spreading, ovate lobes. The lower lip is spotted pale red at the base.

144
145

146

The North American species, *M. moschatus,* is often grown in gardens and has smaller flowers and sticky, glandular stems. Very apt is the name of the genus, derived from the Latin word *mimus* meaning actor or imitator, for the appearance of the corolla suggests a gape or grimace.

Water Lettuce (146) is a typical plant of still and slow-flowing water in the tropics. Its name, *Pistia stratiotes* L. derived from the Greek word *pistos* meaning watery, indicates that it is an aquatic plant. The floating leaf rosettes are composed of stalkless, partly erect, entire leaves, coloured greyish-green with 7 to 15 prominent longitudinal veins and fine, short, woolly hairs in between. They either float on the water or form a striking cornucopia. From the centre of the rosette rises a two-flowered inflorescence enclosed in a spathe. The flowers are small and green with two stamens and a single carpel bearing a great many ovules. Like most aquatic plants distributed in tropical regions throughout the world this species is extremely variable. Several varieties have already been described, for instance var. *spathulata,* var. *obcordata,* differing mostly in the

144

arrangement and shape of the leaves. It is interesting to note that this plant is very ancient, having been found in Tertiary fossil deposits in North America.

Least Reedmace (147) is a bog and waterside herb growing only in water or waterlogged soil. It has a stout creeping rhizome which bears erect stems approximately 75 cm high with linear leaves at the base; the top of the stem is usually leafless. The terminal inflorescence is composed of two cylindrical spadices, usually touching or close together. Both are the same length and are coloured chestnut brown. The top spadix contains only male flowers that soon fall, the bottom spadix is composed of female flowers subtended by bracts — these are persistent. The fruit is unusual, an achene with a long stalk covered with long hairs. The individual species of the genus *Typha* differ in their water-level requirements. Most are to be found in the broad shoreline zone where they are a prominent component of the shoreline vegetation. They often form large masses at the edges of ponds.

Typha minima
Hoppe

147

Gipsywort (148) is usually encountered in waterside thickets, reedbeds, damp ditches and damp
Lycopus europaeus L.   soil in riverine woods. The stem, more than 1 metre high, is covered
with sessile leaves, deeply-toothed on the margin and becoming
increasingly smaller towards the top of the stem. The flowers, arranged
in dense axillary pseudowhorls, are stalkless and small with a bell-
shaped calyx and a bilabiate corolla; the upper lip is two-lobed and
white, the lower lip three-lobed and spotted red. Gipsywort is distributed throughout all Europe from the Azores to the Caucasus, in central
Asia and in middle Siberia. The leaves, which contain the substance
lycopine, were used in folk medicine in medieval days in the form of
a decoction to treat malaria.

148

149

Marsh Woundwort (149) is found in waterside thickets, damp ditches, inundated riverine woods
Stachys palustris L. and as a weed in wet fields. The stem is covered with leaves along its
entire length. The flowers, arranged in a non-contiguous terminal ra-
ceme, grow from the axils of the upper or middle leaves. The corolla is
two-lipped with a long corolla tube slanting downwards; it is greyish-
violet and the bottom lip is covered with dark spots. Marsh Woundwort is distributed throughout all Europe and in Asia to Lake Baikal in
middle Siberia; it occurs sporadically in central Asia and even in Kashmir. Because of its great adaptability it readily invades field crops,
chiefly where the soil is loamy-sandy and permanently moist. Cultivated in Japan for its tuberous rhizomes is the related *S. sieboldii.*

150

151

Carex gracilis Curtis (150) is a prominent sedge species of swampy shorelines and marshy meadows and is also widespread on river banks. The stems, up to 1 metre high, form striking, green 'grass-like' masses. Growing from a stout, creeping rhizome, they are slender, sharp-edged and rough with flat leaves grooved down the middle. They are terminated by racemose inflorescences composed of slender male spikes at the top (these have prominent brown anthers) and female spikes at the bottom (these have conspicuous white stigmas). In late spring, after the flowers are spent, the plant continues to grow, the male spikes dry out and the mature female spikes droop. There are a great variety of sedge species and these plants are well able to adapt to changing conditions in the broad zone of a muddy shore.

Cyperus Sedge (151) is found at the edges of ponds and pools and often in muddy soil with lots
Carex pseudocyperus L. of humus that is continually washed with slow-flowing water. It makes large clumps of yellow-green stems and leaves. The terminal flower spikes are of two kinds, male spikes at the top and cylindrical female spikes at the bottom; the latter have long, pendant stalks. Of the marsh sedges this one is not sufficiently appreciated for the beauty of its shapely inflorescences, whose size and yellow-green colouring are very striking.

Water Crowfoot (152) is found in still and slow-flowing water and often forms large spreading
Ranunculus aquatilis L. masses, chiefly in ponds. The flowers are long-stalked and conspicuous from a distance. This species is characterized by having leaves of different forms on the same stem (heterophylly): floating leaves roundly heart-shaped in outline and submerged leaves finely dissected into thread-like leaflets that fall together like a brush when out of water. This species also thrives in damp mud, but then it produces only one type of leaf with an undivided, orbicular blade. It is distributed throughout all Eurasia and North America from 70° latitude North southward to about level with Europe's Mediterranean region. It is also found in South America, South Africa and Australia.

152

Bog Arum (153) is a plant of muddy, wet soil and shallow still water. It is generally found in wet
Calla palustris L.   alder groves near drainage ditches below pond weirs, where it tolerates even lengthy submersion in water. Rising from the hollow cylindrical rhizome are leafless stems terminated by a lovely spathe, coloured greenish outside and white inside and enclosing a yellow-green spadix of tiny flowers. The fruits are coral-red berries. The leaves are long-stalked and rounded heart-shaped in outline with short-pointed tips. They are conspicuous from afar for they jut above the water and are relatively large.

153

154

Yellow Flag (154) grows mainly in very wet situations — in waterside thickets at the edge of *Iris pseudacorus* L. flowing water or on the muddy shores of ponds, in riverine woods, and often also by woodland pools and in damp ditches — generally in groups. The stem, growing from a thick rhizome, is branched and fresh green in colour, as are the sword-shaped leaves, which are usually the same length as the flowering stems. The flowers are long-stalked and subtended by membranous bracts. The perianth segments are bright yellow, dark yellow in the middle and patterned with violet-brown veins. The rhizomes were used in folk medicine to check bleeding. In Europe, Yellow Flag has a continuous distribution extending eastward to the Urals, northward to the Arctic Circle and southward through the Mediterranean region to northern Africa and Asia Minor.

155

Yellow Loosestrife (155) generally grows alongside rivers and streams where it forms character-
Lysimachia vulgaris L. istic gleaming golden-yellow borders in the summer months. It is also found in waterside thickets, inundated riverine woods and on moorlands. The robust stem grows from a creeping rhizome. The leaves are short-stalked, longish-ovate, dotted with red and with visible veining. The inflorescences grow from the axils of the upper leaves. The flowers have red-edged sepals and yellow petals. This species has a continuous distribution from the British Isles throughout Eurasia (north to the Arctic Circle) to Japan. It was introduced to the Mediterranean region and China. The genus *Lysimachia* also includes species that are often grown as ornamentals for their large yellow flowers.

Policeman's Helmet (156) is an annual herb from the south Asian tropics and subtropics. It is *Impatiens glandulifera* Royle extremely vigorous and rapidly becomes established in new habitats. During the past several decades it has been spreading widely in Europe in waterside thickets by water courses, where it forms continuous masses. The stems are stout, up to 2 metres high, thickened at the nodes and branched. The leaves are ovate, pointed, with a short stalk. The flowers are arranged in long-stalked axillary racemes and measure up to 4 cm across. A characteristic feature are the club-shaped capsules that split at the touch when ripe.

156

Touch-me-not, Jewelweed (157) is a plant of waterside thickets, shaded clearings and moist,
Impatiens mossy edges of woodland streams, favouring places where it does not
noli-tangere L. face strong competition from other species. Characteristically, this
plant forms large spreading masses in partially shaded, damp places.
However, as soon as its habitat is disrupted, for instance by opening of
the tree canopy, it rapidly retreats. The flowers, arranged in axillary
racemes, are large, up to 4 cm long, and long-stalked with a spurred
calyx. The corolla is yellow dotted with red inside. Ripe capsules are
very sensitive to the touch, the valves contracting abruptly to eject the
seeds when the capsules collide, for example when swayed by a strong
wind. The genus *Impatiens* also includes the Yellow Small-flowered
Balsam *(I. parviflora)* which is another woodland plant.

158

Soapwort, Bouncing Bet (158) is found in waterside thickets where it grows in moist or wet *Saponaria officinalis* L. sandy-loamy soils by streams and rivers. The stems are thick, up to 1 metre high and branched in the upper half with opposite, broadly-elongate leaves that are conspicuously three-veined, covered with scattered hairs and rough on the margin. The petals are white to pinkish and shallowly-notched. The pistil develops into a longish-ovoid capsule. The root contains saponins which form a soapy foam when dissolved in water, a fact reflected in the plant's generic name. Double forms are grown in gardens and have purplish red flowers that bloom the whole summer long. Many species of the genus *Saponaria* grow in the mountains of southern Europe and several are popular rock garden plants.

Chapter 6　　ARCTIC-ALPINE PLANTS

Plants with distributions confined to the northern regions and to the mountain ranges of the temperate regions of the northern hemisphere are called arctic-alpine plants. Some grow in Europe or even throughout Eurasia, some in North America, and some have a circumpolar distribution. The northern limit of their range in Europe is approximately 79° North, and in the high mountains of central Europe and North America we will find the same species up to elevations of approximately 3,000 metres, where they find more or less the same conditions for growth as in the arctic regions.

The original homes of these plants were the arctic regions of Europe, Asia and North America, whence they spread during the periods of glaciation to the subalpine and alpine belts of mountain ranges such as the Pyrenees, Alps and Carpathians where they have survived as glacial relics to this day. Many have a large, even though discontinuous distribution. If we were to study all their natural habitats we would have to undertake a lengthy journey not only throughout the whole temperate zone of the northern hemisphere and the arctic region but also through the South American Andes from Colombia to Tierra del Fuego, the North American Rocky Mountains, and the towering Himalayas, including all the high mountains of Asia from Hindukush and Pamir to the volcanoes of Kamchatka and Japan. It is evident that in such an extensive range one species may be marked by great diversity. Its occurrence may be influenced by different climatic, orographic or vegetational conditions as well as by various rock substrates.

Such species may be so variable that they occur as a great many geographico-ecological strains amongst which we often find transitional atypical individuals. And it is the very diversity of these plants that contributes to the scenic beauty of the high mountains and far north. All the more so in that their low, compact cushions smothered with bright glowing flowers generally occur in large numbers. Many blossom at the same time, often in the short spring time of the mountains or the arctic region.

All these attractive wild plants, be they found in high inaccessible mountains or northern tundra, should be protected against all disruptive and harmful factors, for they grow in regions that even in our day and age still remain largely unaffected by the inroads of civilization. This

160

161

chapter includes species many of which are still plentiful in their natural habitats and others that are very rare — all, however, are very colourful and it is difficult to imagine mountain or northern scenery without them.

Included here also are species that are found only in the mountain ranges of Europe, Asia and North America and do not extend to the arctic regions. The distribution and presence of these plants at high altitudes indicates that they have the same requirements as the arctic-alpine species.

Spring Gentian (159) has short stems, each terminated by a single flower. The basal leaves are
Gentiana verna L. arranged in a ground rosette, the stem leaves in pairs, two to three to a stem. The flower is hypocrateriform, consisting of a long tubular calyx and wide-spreading corolla lobes. This gentian grows in mountain districts, generally forming carpets in mountain meadows and pastureland; it is likewise found on grassy rock ledges and in rock crevices and very occasionally it also flowers in lower hilly districts. The flowers are very attractive and vividly coloured. This gentian is distributed

in Europe from the Pyrenees through the Alps, western and southern Carpathians intermittently to the Balkans. In all mountain ranges it favours limestone and dolomite rock substrates.

Gentiana frigida Haenke (160) is a low-growing gentian with glabrous, unbranched stems rising from a thick rhizome. The leaves are narrow, entire, with blunt tips and a short sheath at the base. The flowers, which grow from the axils of the uppermost leaves, have a bell-shaped calyx with five narrow lobes. The corolla is also bell-shaped but with short broad lobes; the colour is not very striking — the petals are pale yellowish-green tipped with pale blue and spotted dark blue. This gentian is one of the hardiest members of the genus and may be found even on very inhospitable rocky substrates at high mountain elevations. It is not very conspicuous in rocky alpine situations with thin grass cover for the pale, soberly coloured flowers merge with the surrounding environment. It is distributed in Europe from the eastern Alps through the western and southern Carpathians to the Rhodopes Mountains in Bulgaria. If we wish to see this rare gentian, then we must make our way to elevations of about 2,000 metres above sea level, to wet rocks and snow fields.

Hungarian Gentian (161) is closely related to the Dotted Gentian (*G. punctata*, species no. 164), from which it differs chiefly by having purple flowers with reddish-black spots. The stem is thick, erect, and up to 75 cm high with broadly ovate to lanceolate leaves. The basal leaves are stalked, the stem

Gentiana pannonica Scop.

162

163

leaves sessile, and the large flowers grow in clusters in the axils of the uppermost leaves. This species is found in mountain pastures and grassy places amidst dwarf pine at mountain to subalpine elevations. It is distributed throughout the central and eastern Alps, whence it extends to northwestern Yugoslavia. The Šumava Mountains of Czechoslovakia mark the northern limit of its range.

Milkweed Gentian (162) is distinguished by fan-like tufts of stems with elliptic, one-veined *Gentiana* leaves, those at the base arranged in two rows on either side of the *asclepiadea* L. stem, those at the top decussate. The large, strikingly coloured flowers with deeply toothed calyces are clustered in the axils of the uppermost leaves. This is an attractive gentian that is often grown in the garden. Its natural habitats are grassy mountain meadows amidst spreads of dwarf pine and open glades and woodland clearings at the forest limit. It is also found beside streams in mountain valleys whence it is washed down to hill districts. Sometimes it may also be encountered in damp, shaded ravines at low elevations where it finds conditions similar to those of its mountain habitat. It grows on a wide variety of rock substrates throughout the temperate regions of Europe from northeastern Spain to the Balkans, being particularly prominent in European mountains. In late summer it is the most striking plant amidst the drying vegetation at higher elevations.

Trumpet or Stemless Gentian (163) has short stems rising from a basal rosette of leathery, pale green leaves and terminated by a single flower up to 6 cm long. The corolla is trumpet-shaped, much larger than that of the Spring Gentian (species no. 159) and thus very striking. It grows in the mountain districts of Europe from the Vosges through the Alps to northwestern Yugoslavia, including the western Carpathians, scattered also in the southern Carpathians. Throughout its range it exhibits a partiality for limestone rock

Gentiana clusii Perr. et Song.

substrates, particularly for grassy expanses on weathering rocks or rocky screes. Truly the epitome of a beautiful mountain flower it rightfully appears as the symbol of protected alpine plants on various emblems and on signs in national parks and nature preserves.

Dotted Gentian (164) is an important species of high mountain elevations where it grows in
Gentiana punctata L.   stony or grassy places often above the dwarf pine belt; however, it may also be found in grass amidst dwarf pine and even in grassy clearings at the edge of closed pine woods. This gentian has a thick rhizome and a stout, erect, hollow stem. The stem leaves are large, broadly ovate, prominently veined and sessile. The large, tubular, bell-shaped flowers grow from the upper leaf axils or at the top of the stem. The corolla is pale yellow with dark violet spots outside. Though there are always several large plants together in one spot they are often indiscernible for the sober colouring of the flowers and leaves makes them blend with the surroundings. The Dotted Gentian is widely distributed in the Alps and western Carpathians, but in the Balkans and southern Carpathians only intermittently.

Crosswort Gentian (165) differs from related species by its robust, thickly leaved stem and in
Gentiana cruciata L.   the number of flowers arranged in clusters in the axils of the middle and uppermost leaves. The leaves are stiff to leathery, the bottom

165

166

leaves fused in pairs by the greater part of their bases. The flowers have a short, bell-shaped calyx and bell-shaped corolla coloured bright blue inside and dingy greenish-blue outside. This gentian grows in hilly districts in dry meadows, woodland margins and open thickets, as well as in mountains, usually in sunny grassy places. It is distributed from the Pyrenees throughout all central and southern Europe to the Urals. The Balkans and Caucasus mark the southern boundary of its range, and northward it extends to the Baltic republics of the U.S.S.R.

White Anemone (166) is one of the first plants to flower in the mountains. The basal as well as
Pulsatilla alba Rchb. stem leaves are deeply cut into narrow, linear segments covered thickly with hairs. The flower stalk lengthens during the flowering period and the flower remains erect with segments expanded until after it is spent. This anemone is found in the mountains of central Europe, in mountain meadows, where it is partial to rather dry places with thick grass cover. It is usually encountered in spreads of mat grass, dwarf pine and by

mountain paths, as a rule on acidic rock substrates, but with the burgeoning of the surrounding vegetation it soon fades into the background. Occasionally one will come across a yellow-flowered specimen and the fruits remain conspicuous even amidst the summer vegetation with their hairy appendages up to 4 cm long.

Bear's-ear Primrose (167) has a stem up to 25 cm high covered with short, fine hairs. The leaves
Primula auricula L. form a basal rosette that is often pressed to the rocky ground. The flower stalk is terminated by an umbel of short-stalked flowers in which the corolla forms a long trumpet with a flared bell of flat, spreading lobes. Another striking feature in addition to the large flowers is the contrast provided by the rosettes of fleshy, grey-green to dark green leaves against the whitish-grey limestone and dolomite rocks on which the plant grows. This species is distributed from the northern and southern perialpine region throughout central Europe to northwestern Yugoslavia. It occurs chiefly on basic rock substrates (limestone and dolomite), mostly in inaccessible places such as steep rock slopes, rocky ledges and overhangs, as well as in cracks and crevices.

167

168

Dwarf Primrose (168) makes low, carpet-like cushions of thick leaf rosettes. It has greatly
Primula minima L. branched rhizomes but no stems. The leaves are stiff with saw-like
teeth and a shining upper surface covered with glandular hairs. The
flowers are very attractive, solitary with stalks up to 3 cm long. The
corolla lobes are spread out flat and cleft about two-thirds to the base.
This species is very well adapted to rugged mountain conditions and
generally grows in rock crevices or on rocky ground with thin grass
cover where there is ample moisture the year round, exhibiting
a preference for noncalcareous substrates. In Europe it is found in the
Alps, Giant (Krkonoše) Mountains, Tatras, southern Carpathians and
randomly in the mountains of the Balkan Peninsula.

169

Primrose (169) grows in meadows, scrub and open woodlands in hilly and foothill districts, its
Primula acaulis (L.) large sulphur-yellow flowers brightening these places in early spring.
Grufb. (syn. *P.* The leaves, arranged in a ground rosette, are glabrous on the upper
vulgaris Huds.) surface, hairy beneath and irregularly, bluntly toothed on the margin.
The flowers with short hairy stalks grow singly from the centre of the
leaf rosettes. The petals are spread out flat and coloured yellow with
an orange blotch at the base, the calyx is green, tubular and winged and
divided almost half-way to the base into five teeth. A characteristic
feature of all yellow-flowered primulas is that they do not have stems.

Mountain Avens (170) is a typical arctic species and is found also in all high mountain regions
Dryas octopetala L. of the north temperate zone except the Himalayas. In Europe its range extends from the Pyrenees through the Alps and Carpathians to the Balkans and the Caucasus, in Asia from the Altai to Lake Baikal; it is also found in the North American Rocky Mountains to California. In the Arctic it has a circumpolar distribution from Alaska through Greenland, Iceland, Scandinavia and the entire Soviet Arctic to Kamchatka — in some places it occurs as far as 80° North. It is partial to limestone and dolomite substrates but is also found on silicic rocks. It forms spreading, cushiony clumps, composed of long, prostrate, branched stems. The leathery leaves are longish-ovate with regularly crenate margins; the upper surface is glossy, the underside white-felted. The flowers, up to 5 cm across, have long downy stalks and are usually composed of eight white petals (a characteristic reflected in the scientific name *octopetala*). The fruits have long hairy appendages.

170

171

Golden Cinquefoil (171) is a plant found in all Europe's high mountain ranges. It occurs chiefly
Potentilla aurea in subalpine and alpine meadows from the Pyrenees through the Alps,
Torner High Sudetens and Carpathians to the mountains of Bulgaria, descending from the stony alpine grasslands and the thin cover of dwarf pine to the edges of mountain spruce woods. Ecologically it is a very adaptable species for it grows both on acidic rocks as well as on limestone and dolomite substrates. The basal leaves growing from the rhizome are positioned alternately opposite each other, an arrangement retained also by the dried remnants of the stipules. The blades of these basal leaves are palmate with five leaflets whereas the stem leaves are trifoliolate. The individual leaflets are silky-hairy on the underside.

Rock Speedwell (172) is a prominent arctic-alpine species occurring chiefly on limestone and
Veronica fruticans
Jacq.
dolomite rocks in high stony mountain pastures (and very occasionally
also on granite substrates). It is found in Europe's high mountains (the
Pyrenees, Alps and Carpathians) and in the arctic region of Finland
and Scandinavia where it extends to 70° North; it is also encountered
in the mountains of Scotland, Iceland and Greenland's southern coast.
Characteristic features include the erect stem with blunt, obovate, glossy leaves, with basal leaves smaller than the upper stem leaves. The
flowers, arranged in a scanty terminal raceme, are stalked and have
deep blue spreading petals with a conspicuous red ring in the centre.

172

Daffodil Anemone (173) has a conspicuously long (up to 50 cm high) and hairy stem. The
Anemone
narcissiflora L.
basal leaves are long-stalked and deeply palmate, being divided into five segments. There are no stem leaves apart from the whorl below the cluster (umbel) of long-stalked flowers. Unlike other anemones which usually have solitary flowers, the blossoms of this species are borne in clusters of three to eight. The Daffodil Anemone is found in grassy screes at higher elevations as well as lower down in alpine grasslands near the forest limit and often also in damp, grassy ditches. It is distributed in the mountains of Europe and Asia and in the far north to the Arctic Circle in arctic tundra communities; it also occurs in similar Alaskan tundra.

Anemone speciosa Ad. (174) is a species typical of the high mountain meadows of the central Caucasus. Its yolk-yellow flowers brighten the grasslands of this mountain range, also appearing in places with slowly melting snow. The perianth segments are broadly ovate, the three- to five-lobed leaves have jagged, toothed margins.

174

175

Twin-flowered Violet or Yellow Wood Violet (175) is an unusual violet in that it is relatively
Viola biflora L.   small and has yellow flowers on long, upright stalks. It is distributed in
Europe from the Pyrenees through the Alps, High Sudetens and Carpathians to the Caucasus and in the north from Norway through all of subarctic Eurasia to Kamchatka; on the American continent it grows in Alaska. It is a damp- and shade-loving plant and hence in mountains it is found in damp sloping meadows, near springs, in wet rock crevices and in the shade of prostrate dwarf pines. In the cold regions of the far north it grows in tundra plant communities up to and even beyond the Arctic Circle. In some parts of its range it descends to lower elevations where conditions suit it.

Mountain Pansy (176)
Viola lutea Huds.
subsp. *sudetica*
(Willd.) Nyman

has unbranched stems with rounded or elliptic, yellow-green leaves and large terminal flowers up to 4 cm in diameter. It is found in the mountains of central Europe — in the Sudetens and western Carpathians. The illustrated subspecies has a larger than average bottom petal with differently coloured markings. In mountain meadows it often occurs in great numbers, sometimes in ring-like clusters, anchoring itself and spreading by means of short runners. Occasionally it crossbreeds with the related mountain species of Heartsease *(V. tricolor* subsp. *subalpina);* the hybrid offspring characteristically have smaller violet-tinged flowers. Interbreeding is quite common amongst members of the genus *Viola,* thus generally making it difficult to distinguish between them.

176

Purple Coltsfoot (177) is readily recognized by the basal rosette of rounded to kidney-shaped, semileathery leaves with crenate margins; they are dark green above and violet-tinged beneath. The flowering stems are terminated by solitary flower heads with large, strikingly coloured strap-shaped ray florets. The snow-white pappus on the achenes makes the plants conspicuous long after the flowers have faded. Purple Coltsfoot is generally found in damp mountain spruce woods, in wet meadows, in grass amidst dwarf pine and near springs in mountain districts, sometimes also in peat meadows at the edge of mountain heaths. It always grows singly, scattered over a large area.

Homogyne alpina Cass.

177

174

178

Fringed Pink (178) is a very shapely plant with robust, faintly pruinose, sparsely branched stems
Dianthus superbus L. and opposite, broadly lanceolate, pointed leaves. Most attractive are
subsp. *alpestris* the large, fragrant flowers. Each is subtended by bracts, which like the
Kablik. ex Čelak. tubular calyx are coloured. The petals are undivided only at the base,
otherwise they are fringed. This pink is found in mountain meadows in
all the mountain ranges of Europe and Asia. It has a continuous distribution from the Pyrenees to the Far East and in northern regions it
extends beyond the Arctic Circle. It is extremely variable and occurs as
different subspecies at various elevations — the illustrated subspecies
alpestris is without a doubt the loveliest of all.

179

Cloudberry (179) is found throughout the whole Arctic region in birchwoods as well as on the
Rubus chamaemorus L. open tundra. It is also to be found in upland and mountain regions of
the more northern parts of Europe, where it represents one of the
surviving relics of the last glaciation. It is a herbaceous species with
five-lobed leaves and unbranched, spineless stems covered with short,
stalked glandular hairs. The flowers, borne singly at the tips of each
stem, are white. As the fruit matures, the stem increases in length and
the whole plant, including the leaves, becomes larger. Because its fruit
resembles that of the Raspberry, Cloudberry is sometimes called 'Raspberry of the North'.

176

Alpine Bellflower (180) is an attractive alpine species with a thick cover of whitish hairs on the stems and flower-stalks. The stems, growing from a basal leaf rosette, are simple, erect, and approximately 20 cm high. Both basal and stem leaves are lanceolate with pointed tips and entire or finely crenate margins. The inflorescence is usually a many-flowered raceme; occasionally, however, it is composed of only two or three flowers. The corolla is broadly funnel-bell-shaped with pointed petals that are fringed inside. This bellflower is found on grassy or stony slopes, on overgrown rocks and often amidst dwarf pine at subalpine elevations from the eastern Alps through the Carpathians to the Balkan mountains, where it occurs as a separate subspecies.

Campanula alpina
Jacq.

180

Common White Hellebore (181) is a robust plant with a stout, densely leaved stem and broadly *Veratrum album* L. elliptical, many-veined, pointed leaves. The racemose inflorescence is subsp. *lobelianum* composed of small, short-stalked, yellow-green flowers. The perianth (Bernh.) Arc. segments are narrow and darkly veined. This plant is noted for its great ecological tolerance (for instance it tolerates a variety of temperatures and moisture conditions), a fact which is reflected also in its vertical distribution. Besides mountain meadows and stony slopes it is also found above stands of dwarf pine. It is likewise encountered on inland steppes and in the north is found beyond the Arctic Circle in subarctic territory. Its range in Europe extends from Spain through central and southern Europe to the Ukrainian steppes, whence it continues on to subarctic Asia and through Siberia to northeastern China. Because it contains toxic substances it is not endangered by the browsing of forest animals nor by herds of cattle.

181

182

Roseroot (182) is a tufted plant up to 40 cm high with a fleshy stem thickly covered with
Rhodiola rosea L.   alternate, lanceolate to longish-ovate leaves. It has a continuous distribution in the northern regions of Europe, Asia and North America but
in the mountains of the north temperate zone it has a disrupted range.
It occurs as a great many varieties differing chiefly in the colour of the
flowers and shape of the leaves. For example the flowers of the European plants are mostly yellow whereas in eastern Asia and Alaska the
prevailing colour of the blossoms is red to violet.

183

Grim the Collier (183) like other hawkweeds, has flower heads furnished with a protective cover
Hieracium of dense glandular hairs. The stalks supporting the flower heads (capi-
aurantiacum L. tula) are likewise thickly covered with black glands so that the bright
hues of the flowers themselves are not revealed until they open. This
species grows in the mountains of western and central Europe and in
Scandinavia. It is also found at lower elevations as a cultivated plant in
rock gardens and is naturalized as an escape. In the wild it may be
encountered in mountain meadows, pastures and high mountain grasslands, often at alpine elevations in Europe's mountains. Many hybrids
exist in the wild, the result of crosses between Grim the Collier and
countless other related species.

Hieracium alpinum L. (184) has densely hairy, glandular stems topped by large solitary heads of strap-shaped flowers. The inflorescence is thickly hairy to woolly and from a distance looks like a fine, thin spiderweb supporting bright yellow corollas with conspicuous yellow styles. Even when not in bloom the plant is readily recognizable because the basal leaves, arranged in a rosette, are thickly covered with minute glands that shimmer in the sun. This species is found in mountain meadows, pastures and screes, chiefly at higher elevations above the forest limit amidst dwarf pine. It is also found in cold northern regions at the level of the Arctic Circle. A notable characteristic of this plant is that in the rugged conditions of its mountain habitats it multiplies only by asexual, (apogamic) means, and consequently exhibits a slightly different form in every small separate locality in which it grows. That is why in literature a great many taxons are grouped together in the broadly embracing species *Hieracium alpinum.*

184

Milk Rock-jasmine (185) has a characteristic ground rosette of clustered, linear-lanceolate
Androsace lactea L. leaves, from the centre of which rises a short, glabrous stem terminated
by an umbel of long-stalked flowers up to 12 mm in diameter. The
petals are white and joined to form a short tube with a wide funnel-
shaped mouth. Sometimes short creeping stems terminated by small
leaf rosettes are found, growing from the main rosette. This plant is
found on limestone and dolomite substrates at subalpine to alpine elevations only in Europe — from the French Jura throughout the northern part of the Alps to the western Carpathians. It occurs sporadically
in the southern Carpathians and in the mountains of northwestern and
central Yugoslavia.

185

186

Chickweed Wintergreen (186) is a typical plant of shaded mountain spruce woods with ample
Trientalis europaea L. ground humus. It also grows in peat soils in hilly districts and subalpine
elevations. It is distributed throughout the entire temperate zone to the
arctic zone of Europe and Asia, from Iceland to Japan approximately
between 45° and 70° latitude North. In North America it is replaced by
the closely related *T. borealis* Raf. The illustrated species has obovate
leaves clustered in a rosette near the top of the erect stems. The latter
are terminated by solitary, stalked, white flowers with parts arranged in
sevens — each has 7 sepals, 7 petals, 7 stamens and 7 carpels.

183

Purple Saxifrage (187) is a very hardy plant found both in the high mountains of the north *Saxifraga oppositifolia* L. temperate zone as well as in northern subarctic regions, usually in rock crevices, on scree and near moraines. It favours shallow soil with herbaceous cover. Noteworthy is the range of its vertical distribution: from sea level near the Arctic Circle to elevations of approximately 5,000 metres in the freezing high mountain semideserts of western Tibet. Throughout this vast range it grows on various rock substrates and tolerates temperatures as low as minus 40° C without a snow cover. The flowers often emerge while the ground is still covered with a thin layer of snow. The leaves, which are opposite, longish-obovate and bristly on the margin, are persistent and remain green throughout the year. Pieces of the stem that break off and are carried by gales or avalanches far from the parent plant root readily thereby contributing to the spread of the species as do the incredibly light seeds (weighing about 0.0001 gram) which are carried great distances by the wind.

187

188

Silver Saxifrage (188) is found on limestone and dolomite rocks and on rocky scree in the
Saxifraga paniculata Pyrenees, Alps, Carpathians, Balkan mountains and Caucasus. In the
Mill. far north it occurs sporadically in Norway, Iceland, southern Greenland and northeastern, subarctic regions of Canada. It is a tufted plant
with a thick, sparsely leaved stem branching at the top. The fleshy,
green-grey basal leaves are arranged in a ground rosette and have
a toothed margin with a lime-secreting gland at the base of each tooth.
This prevents excessive evaporation of water and is a typical characteristic of this species. The flowers, arranged in raceme-like inflorescences, have spreading, glandular stalks and petals usually coloured white,
occasionally spotted with red.

185

189

Alpine Rock-cress (-189) is found on the stony banks of mountain streams or springs and in
Arabis alpina L. damp places on the arctic tundra, more commonly on calcareous substrates. The basal leaf rosette gives rise to a thickly hairy, sparsely
leaved stem and the leaves are ovate with coarsely toothed margins.
The flowers have white petals and are arranged in a dense terminal
raceme. The fruits have stalks perpendicular to the main axis of the
infructescence. Alpine Rock-cress is distributed throughout the high
mountains of Europe from the Pyrenees to the Balkan Peninsula and
eastward through Asia Minor to the Caucasus; it is also found in the

Atlas Mountains of north Africa. In the north, where its range extends almost to 80° North, it is distributed from the Atlantic region of the Canadian Arctic through southern Greenland, Iceland and Spitzbergen (Svalbard) to the mountains of Scandinavia and eastward to the arctic Urals region. The double form is often grown in the rock garden.

Swallowwort (190) has
Vincetoxicum
hirundinaria Med.
a stem up to 1 metre high covered with opposite leaves and terminated by umbel-like inflorescences of white or yellowish flowers. The bottom leaves are broadly heart-shaped, ovate, the upper leaves narrowly lanceolate; all have pubescent veins on the underside. Swallowwort is a photophilic plant partial to dry, rocky or grassy slopes on volcanic rock substrates from lowland to mountain elevations. It is distributed throughout all Europe from northern Spain to the Urals as well as in western Siberia. In the south it is common throughout the whole Mediterranean region, in the north it extends only to southern Sweden.

190

191

Mountain Houseleek (191) has fleshy stems covered with very fleshy leaves affixed by broad bases to the stem. The terminal inflorescences are composed of as many as eight short-stalked flowers each with a reddish, glandular pubescent calyx. The petals are linear, bright reddish-rose and covered with white hairs outside. The corolla is of varied hues, influenced, no doubt, by the respective rock substrates and elevation. Mountain Houseleek is found throughout the European Alps and randomly in the western and southern Carpathians where it occurs as a slightly different form designated var. *carpaticum* Wettst. When not in flower the thick, globose or flattened, fleshy-leaved rosettes look like tiny 'mountain cabbages'. They usually grow on stony mountain grasslands, screes and in damp rock crevices. Mountain Houseleek multiplies by means of long shoots that root readily and rapidly in the inhospitable rocky terrain, as evidenced by the presence of its many tiny leaf rosettes.

*Sempervivum
montanum* L.

Members of the genus *Sempervivum* are succulents found in the temperate regions of the northern hemisphere.

188

Houseleek (192) differs from the Mountain Houseleek (*Sempervivum montanum* — species no.
Sempervivum hirtum 191) primarily in the colour of the flowers and in its preference for
Juslen. limestone and dolomite substrates, though it is also found on silicic
rocks. The leafy, fleshy stem, growing from a large ground rosette of
fleshy, broadly ovate leaves, is glandular-hairy along its entire length
and the stem leaves are thinly ciliate on the margins. The flowers, on
short glandular stalks, are arranged in a thick terminal cluster about
8 cm across. This plant grows on rocks, screes and stony slopes at
mountain to alpine elevations in the eastern Alps and western Carpathians. From the Alps it extends to northwestern Yugoslavia.

192

Snowdon Lily (193) is a bulbous plant with a slender stem, usually 15 cm high. Characteristic *Lloydia serotina* (L.) Rchb features are the two linear basal leaves which are longer than the stem. The stem leaves are short and linear-lanceolate. The flowers are solitary, upward facing and broadly funnel-shaped, and up to 15 mm across; the petals are white with reddish or purplish veins. This species is found on damp rocks and in stony high-mountain meadows at alpine elevations in the Alps, Carpathians and Caucasus; in Asia it extends from Pamir southeast through the Himalayas and northwest to the Baikal region. It occurs in arctic tundra communities continuously from the Urals to Kamchatka, and in northern Japan and Sakhalin. In North America it is distributed from Alaska southward through the Rocky Mountains to California.

193

194

Chives (194) is a high mountain plant found in wet meadows, near springs and in wet rock
Allium crevices from the Alps to eastern Asia. It may also be encountered
schoenoprasum L. throughout the subarctic regions of Europe, Asia and North America.
subsp. *sibiricum* (L.) This subspecies has a more robust habit with more compressed leaves
Hartman than the kitchen herb of the same name, which forms another subspecies growing at lower elevations. The perianth segments of mountain
populations are linear lanceolate and coloured deep pink; a typical
characteristic is the globose shape of the inflorescence and the sparsely
leaved stem. Like other species of *Allium* this high mountain plant is
readily recognized by its penetrating aroma.

Clusius's Leopardsbane (195) with its large flower heads up to 6 cm across, is a striking plant of
Doronicum clusii grassy and stony slopes in European mountains at subalpine to alpine
(All.) Tausch. elevations. The stem is simple and erect, sparsely leaved and hairy; the
upper half is glandular. The leaves are elliptical with toothed margins

191

195

— the basal leaves are stalked, the stem leaves sessile and pressed against the stem by their heart-shaped bases. This species is distributed from the mountains of the Iberian Peninsula through the Pyrenees, Alps and entire Carpathian massif to the southern Carpathians. The plants from the eastern part of the Alps and the Carpathians are classed as a separate subspecies (ssp. *villosum*), for the leaf surfaces of these plants are thickly covered with hairs.

Edelweiss, Lion's-foot
Leontopodium
alpinum Cass.

(196, 197) is an important species of Europe's high mountain ranges distributed from the Pyrenees through the Alps and Carpathians to the Balkan Peninsula and on through the Caucasus to the mountain regions of central Asia. It is a characteristic plant of limestone and dolomite substrates and is found solely in rocky situations or on grassy screes, often in exposed, inaccessible places. It catches the eye from afar with

196

its white-woolly appearance, for all parts of the plant are covered with wool — the stem, leaves and bracts as well as the flower heads. The small semiglobose heads are subtended by spreading white-woolly petal-like bracts of unequal size arranged in a star-like pattern. This is a popular rock garden plant, though sometimes it is unsuitably planted out at lower elevations. Like certain species of gentian it has become a popular symbol of conservationists.

197

Red Campion (198) has a branched stem with soft hairs and opposite, sessile, broadly elliptic, *Silene dioica* Clairv. shortly hairy leaves. The flowers are clustered in terminal racemes on short stalks and have an inflated, veined calyx. A striking characteristic of this plant is that the flowers open fully only in full sun. Red Campion is found in wet meadows, woodland margins, open woods and often also in damp roadside ditches and by the wayside, particularly in piedmont and mountain districts. It has a continuous distribution throughout all Europe excepting the southernmost Mediterranean region. In the north it extends along the coast of Norway up to and above the Arctic Circle.

198

199

Moss Campion (199) is a perennial with very short stems and small rosettes of short, linear-lan-
Silene acaulis (L.) ceolate leaves, shortly ciliate on the margin. From the centre of the leaf
Jacq. rosette grows a single stalkless or short-stalked flower. The petals are
two-lobed and often of variable colour. Moss Campion forms flat cushions or spreading carpets typically found in extreme locations such as
rock overhangs, rock ledges and rock crevices as well as in shallow
stony soils on both limestone and acidic siliceous rock substrates.
Plants growing on such diverse substrates, however, naturally exhibit
slight differences. The illustrated species occurs in the Alps, Carpathians and mountains of the Balkan Peninsula and is also distributed in the
northern parts of Europe, Asia and America, including the subarctic
islands.

200

Marsh Andromeda (200) has narrow, linear-lanceolate leaves with revolute margins and
Andromeda polifolia L. a greyish-pruinose undersurface. The long-stalked, nodding flowers are
arranged in a scanty corymbose cluster at the upright tip of the upright
section of the otherwise prostrate stem. Each flower has a pale pink
flask-like corolla divided at the tip into short, recurved, red lobes.
Marsh Andromeda is found on submontane and high moors at mountain to alpine elevations; it often grows in moist sphagnum-bogs. It has
a continuous circumpolar distribution throughout the northern hemisphere, being a common element of tundra vegetation from 50° to 70°
North in Europe, Asia and North America. It is also found in the Alps,
Carpathians and Scottish mountains.

Carpathian Soldanella (201) has prominently rounded kidney-shaped leaves arranged in
Soldanella carpatica a ground rosette. They are fleshy with a crenate margin, dark green
Vierh. above and reddish on the underside. Older leaves are slightly wrinkled
with a revolute margin and a glandular stalk. The flowering stems,
covered with minute glands, are terminated by drooping, blue, bell-
shaped flowers with the corolla cut almost half-way to the base into
narrow slender lobes. Carpathian Soldanella usually grows above the
forest limit, mostly amidst dwarf pine in the vicinity of springs and in
grassy places that remain wet a long time as the snow slowly melts. It
also grows in rock crevices which are shaded and moist in summer. It is
found in central Europe in the western Carpathians, usually on noncalcareous substrates.

201

Bog Bilberry (202) is a robust shrub up to 75 cm high with creeping stems and erect, glabrous twigs. The leaves are ovate with entire revolute margins and prominent veins. The grey-green upper surface of the leaves distinguishes this plant from the related Common Bilberry *(V. myrtillus)*. The flask-like flowers are nodding and clustered in scanty racemes. The globose berries are edible but if eaten in large quantities cause headache and vomiting. The Bog Bilberry is found on submontane moors and heaths as well as on high moors at mountain to subalpine elevations and in the northern tundra. Its range in Europe extends from the Pyrenees through the Alps to the Carpathians and, except in western Europe, continuously northward to above the Arctic Circle. In Asia and North America it has a continuous distribution from 50° to 80° North.

Vaccinium uliginosum L.

202

203

Achyrophorus uniflorus (Vill.) Bluff et Fingerh. (203) has stout, unbranched, leafless stems covered with bristly hairs and conspicuously swollen beneath the flower heads. The leaves are generally arranged in a basal rosette, though sometimes there are several leaves on the lower part of the stem. The large terminal flower head, up to 6 cm in diameter, is composed only of strap-shaped flowers. The involucral bracts beneath the flower head are covered with black hairs. This plant is found in high mountains throughout all Eurasia, from the Alps to Japan, and also in the mountains of North and South America. Occurring in such a vast range it is naturally quite variable, chiefly in the shape of the leaf and size of the flower head. It grows predominantly on siliceous substrates.

204

Alpine-sanicle (204) has a glandular-hairy stem up to 50 cm high terminated by an umbel com-
Cortusa matthioli L. posed of as many as twelve flowers. The leaves, arranged in a ground
rosette, are long-stalked and roundly kidney-shaped with saw-toothed
lobes. This species is generally found in mountain meadows, on partly
overgrown screes, in shaded gullies and on mossy rocks facing away
from the sun. It appears to be most common in places where snow
remains on the ground till late spring. The plant is named after the
Italian botanist J. A. Cortusi and P. A. Matthioli, author of the famous
16th century herbal. In the northern hemisphere there are several related species, the large-flowered varieties of which are grown as ornamentals in the garden.

Brown Trefoil (205) is a biennial or perennial plant with branched stems covered with ap-
Trifolium badium pressed hairs. The leaves are long-stalked and trifoliolate. The inflores-
Schreb. cence is a long-stalked head (capitulum) of many flowers. The indivi-
dual flowers have a tubular calyx and the corolla has one petal larger

than the rest which determines the colouration of the whole cluster and which is swollen and spoon-shaped. This species is found at higher mountain elevations chiefly on limestone, dolomite and other basic rock substrates. It grows near springs, in grassy screes, and on stony slopes throughout Europe — from the Pyrenees, through the Alps, Apennine Peninsula, western, eastern and southern Carpathians to the mountains of Bulgaria. It is an exception within the genus *Trifolium* to which it belongs, for of the many species embraced within the genus only a few grow in the mountains.

Alpine Aster (illustrated on page 6) usually has unbranched, shortly hairy stems with long-
Aster alpinus L.　　ish, hairy, conspicuously three-veined leaves. The flower heads at the tops of the stems have golden-yellow disc florets and large ray florets coloured violet-blue or pink to white. A characteristic of this species is marked variation in the colour of the flowers, a factor which may be influenced by the rock substrate. This aster is often found on exposed, inaccessible, rocky cliffs, in rock crevices and on the edges of rock overhangs, as well as on screes with thin grass cover. It grows primarily on limestone, dolomite and other basic rock substrates, not only in mountain districts but also in piedmont and foothill districts, often at the bottom of deep shaded ravines.

205

Chapter 7

SYMBIOTIC AND PARASITIC PLANTS

Most plants obtain their food by the process known as photosynthesis, that is they combine carbon dioxide and water to form sugars using sunlight, trapped by their chlorophyll, as a source of energy. However, not all plants have this ability and these others must obtain their food by other means; they are known as mixotrophic plants. Plants such as the carnivorous plants described in Chapter 3 are only partially mixotrophic, others are wholly mixotrophic. The mycorrhiza found in the roots of orchids are an example of this latter group.

All plants that exist in this way are modified in both shape and structure to better adapt them for the lives they lead. The most striking example of how plants are affected by their means of subsistence are the parasitic plants which draw their sustenance (organic substances) from the host. Such plants are often coloured other than green and their leaves are greatly reduced, as are the roots and the woody parts of the vascular bundles. On the other hand they have root-like outgrowths called haustoria through which they absorb water (and the minerals dissolved therein) as well as food from the conducting tissues of the green plants that are their hosts. Examples are various species of broomrape and toothwort. Many parasitic plants are 'specialists' in terms of host as well as nitrogen-compound requirements.

Hemiparasitism is a means of subsistence characteristic of many autotrophic vascular plants growing in nitrogen-deficient soils, for instance in pastureland on podzol or in wet meadows. These plants cling with their roots to the roots of other plants in meadow communities. Typical examples are certain members of the figwort family, such as Cow-wheat, Yellow-rattle, and Lousewort. It is a fact that even hemiparasitism affects the morphological and anatomical characteristics of these plants, albeit in lesser degree.

Toothwort (206, 208) has a stout, branched underground rhizome covered with white scales
Lathraea squamaria L. from which rises a glabrous, fleshy and flesh-coloured stem. The stem
is covered with scale-like rounded, pointed leaves with heart-shaped

207

bases that are markedly smaller towards the top of the stem and are coloured white or pale pink. The plant's most striking feature are the flowers, arranged in a dense, one-sided terminal raceme that is pendulous at first. They have a glandular-hairy calyx and tubular funnel-shaped bilabiate corolla coloured pale pink with a conspicuously reddish lower lip. Lacking green colouring, the plant feeds solely by parasitic means. It grows in damp leafy soil in shaded broad-leaved woods where it is a striking element in spring when the forest floor is not yet carpeted with a spreading herb layer. This species is distributed throughout practically all Europe from the British Isles to the western Ukraine and from the Mediterranean region to central Scandinavia.

Clove-scented Broomrape (207) is generally parasitic on bedstraw (genus *Galium*). It has no
Orobanche
caryophyllacea
Smith
chlorophyll. The stem is simple, glandular-pubescent and swollen like a tuber at the base near the ground. The scale-like leaves are few in number and arranged alternately on the stem. The flowers, clustered in dense terminal racemes, grow from the axils of the leaves. This species is found on dry sunny slopes, particularly on volcanic rock substrates, throughout all Europe — from France to the central Ukraine, including the Mediterranean region. It belongs to a genus that includes a great many species parasitic on widely diverse dicotyledonous as well as monocotyledonous plants. Most, however, are parasitic only on a certain species, group of species or family.

208

209

Common Wintergreen (209) is a perennial green plant with rounded, stalked leaves arranged in
Pyrola minor L.　　a basal rosette. The flowering stem is leafless, covered only with a few
scales and terminated by a scanty racemose inflorescence. The flowers
have a globular white or pale pink corolla. The plant's occurrence is
dependent on the presence of symbiotic mycorrhizal fungi, which find
woodland soil most congenial for growth. The symbiotic association
between the two is of mutual benefit without limiting the wintergreen's
normal production of food by photosynthesis. The Common Wintergreen is distributed throughout the northern hemisphere, in North
America, Europe and Asia, being found chiefly in open, mossy forest
margins and open coniferous woods from lowland to mountain districts. It is generally encountered in places where there is less competi-

210

tion from companion herbaceous species and is common in tundra communities in subarctic regions where it extends beyond the Arctic Circle.

Alpine Bartsia (210) is
Bartsia alpina L.
a hemiparasitic species with a creeping rhizome and unbranched stems covered with random hairs. The stem leaves are ovate with notched margins, nearly sessile and shortly hairy on the upper surface; the lowermost leaves resemble scales. The flowers grow from the upper leaf axils and are arranged in terminal spikes. The calyx is bell-shaped and woolly, the corolla tubular funnel-shaped. This species grows in mountains at subalpine and alpine elevations, generally in rather damp grassy places amidst dwarf pine, alongside mountain streams and springs and on wet, moss-covered rocky ground above the forest limit. It is distributed in European mountains from the Pyrenees through the Alps to the southern Carpathians and it also occurs in the subarctic regions of Scandinavia including the Kola Peninsula. In the western

hemisphere its range extends from southern Greenland to the north-eastern part of subarctic Canada.

Blue-topped Cow-wheat (211) is readily identified not only by its opposite sessile leaves but chiefly by its strikingly coloured, deeply toothed bracts and flowers clustered in dense terminal spikes. The individual flowers grow from the axils of the bracts, which form a colourful crest at the top of the stems. The calyx is tubular, the corolla funnel-shaped and two-lipped, the upper lip galeate (helmet-shaped), the lower lip flat. Cow-wheat grows in open broad-leaved woods, woodland margins and in grassy hedgerows in lowland and hilly country. Though it contains chlorophyll it is occasionally parasitic on the underground parts of other green plants in whose company it grows and is thus a hemiparasite. It is distributed in the temperate and northern parts of Europe, approximately from Germany to the central Urals and from the central Mediterranean region to southern Sweden.

Melampyrum
nemorosum L.

211

Whorled Lousewort (212) forms tufts of stems growing from a basal rosette of leaves. The stem *Pedicularis verticillata* L. leaves are whorled and both they and the leaves are pinnate, divided into minute ovate segments and covered with hairs. The flowers are violet and clustered in terminal spikes at the tops of the stems. The size and colourfulness of the inflorescence is underscored by the violet-tinged bracts. Whorled Lousewort grows in high mountain ranges at subalpine and alpine elevations in damp grassy places, mossy rock crevices, beside springs and often near snow fields. In Europe its range extends from the Pyrenees to the southern Carpathians and, though absent in the vast expanses of northern Canada, it has a continuous distribution throughout the subarctic zone of the northern hemisphere. Like the preceding species it is a hemiparasite. Mountain species of lousewort are hemiparasitic chiefly on certain plants of the pea family, many of which occur as subalpine or alpine species.

Common Yellow-rattle (213), like the preceding species, is a hemiparasite. Its erect, four-angled *Rhinanthus minor* L. stems are covered with opposite, sessile leaves with serrate margins and topped by a spike-like inflorescence of strikingly large flowers —

212

213

large due to the persistent, green calyces, each inflated into a globose shape. The corolla is pale yellow and two-lipped with a long corolla tube and a helmet-shaped upper lip. This species is most common in moderately dry meadows, woodland clearings and pastureland and is found from lowland to mountain districts. It is extremely variable, particularly in the branching of the stems and number of stem segments — undoubtedly due to the diverse ecological conditions of its habitats and its vertical distribution. It is distributed from the temperate to the subarctic zone of the northern hemisphere, from Greenland throughout all Europe to western Siberia and in the subarctic regions to 70° latitude North.

Chapter 8   COMPOSITE FLOWERS

Plants of the family Compositae vary greatly in appearance, occur in widely diverse habitats, are popular ornamentals and include medicinal herbs as well as plants of economic importance. They have a worldwide distribution but are most numerous in North America and are readily identified by the unique structure of the inflorescence. This is called a head or anthodium which, although it looks as if it is a single flower, is in reality a dense, flattened cluster of a great many sessile flowers attached to a common receptacle with a prominent involucre. The blossoms of the sunflower, daisy, dandelion and hawkweed all appear to be similar, differing only in size or colouration. There are, however, basic differences between them. The heads of the sunflower and daisy, for example, consist of a central disc composed of tubular flowers and a margin composed of strap-shaped or ligulate flowers (cultivated species also include 'double' forms), whereas the heads of dandelion and hawkweed comprise only strap-shaped flowers. There are, of course, other features of identification that are characteristic of these plants, for instance the presence of oil ducts in the leaves and stems, lactiferous ducts in the plant tissues, and underground parts that are either tuberous or rhizomatous. Different species of composite plants are eaten as vegetables, provide drugs or are grown for their decorative effect. They are remarkable in that when in full bloom their huge inflorescences often remain fresh for a long time. The fruits, which are produced in large quantities, are in some instances furnished with a striking white pappus, in others with a spike-like or hooked appendage. Only a fraction, however, develop into new plants.

Jerusalem Artichoke (214) grows from underground tubers which are well known as
Helianthus tuberosus L. a delicately flavoured potato-like vegetable. The stems are very rough along their entire length and felted below the flower head. The leaves are long-stalked and conspicuously toothed on the margins. The heads are up to 8 cm in diameter and composed of tubular disc florets and

215

large marginal strap-shaped florets up to 3 cm long. The involucre is ciliate and composed of several rows of bracts. The fruits are furnished with several awns. Plants of the genus *Helianthus* are generally found in North America, occasionally also in Central America to Peru. All are of robust habit and have large flower heads.

Daisy-star Aster (215) grows on rather moist stony ground, especially on limestone, in Europe's
Aster bellidiastrum mountain regions whence in congenial situations, for instance damp
(L.) Scop. (syn. shaded ravines, it often descends to lower elevations. It has a basal
Bellidiastrum rosette of elliptical, short-stalked leaves with toothed margins from
michelii Cass.) which rises a downy stem topped by a solitary head. The leaves are randomly hairy on the upper surface and downy beneath, particularly along the veins. The flower head measures up to 4 cm in diameter and has narrow ray florets.

Daisy (216) is a small perennial found in grassy places throughout the northern hemisphere. Its
Bellis perennis L. flowers are a pretty sight in fresh green turf and drier meadows in spring and once again in early autumn amidst the drying vegetation following the lush growth of summer. From the basal leaf rosette rises a stem up to 15 cm high terminated by a solitary head with yellow disc florets and white pink-tinged ray florets. Cultivated forms (cultivars) with large heads are grown in gardens as annuals. 'Ligulosa' is the

216

217

name given to double cultivars with heads composed only of ligulate florets and 'Fistulosa' the name given to those with only tubular florets. The Daisy has been used in folk medicine since time immemorial — chiefly for its beneficial effects in the treatment of dermatitis and diseases of the upper respiratory passages. The dried leaves were added to tea mixtures, mainly to enhance their appearance. The genus *Bellis* includes approximately 8 species distributed throughout the northern hemisphere from lowland to mountain elevations. The separate species are quite similar, differing chiefly in the size and colour of the flower heads and in the period of flowering.

Chicory (217) is a typical plant of fallow land, pastures, grassy hedgerows and waysides from
Cichorium intybus L. lowland to foothill districts. Its large attractive heads are composed of bisexual ligulate florets and their bright blue colour makes them con-

213

218

spicuous from afar, though sometimes they may be white or pale pink. The fruits are without a pappus and are terminated by bristle-like appendages. Chicory was formerly used in folk medicine chiefly in treating liver diseases. The roots of cultivated Chicory are also used as a coffee substitute, which, however, lacks the characteristic pleasant taste and stimulant action of coffee and resembles it only in colour; the tender young leaves are used in salads.

Yellow Chamomile (218) has erect, woolly, leafy stems branching sparsely in the upper half. *Anthemis tinctoria* L. The leaves are divided into small segments. The stem is terminated by a solitary head 2 to 4 cm in diameter with a raised conical receptacle and disc and ray florets of the same colour; in older heads the ray florets droop. This chamomile is found in sunny, rocky places, chiefly on volcanic rock substrates, though it also grows on silicic substrates. Many related species, most with white ray florets, are found chiefly in Europe's Mediterranean region where they grow as weeds.

Senecio nemorensis L. (219) has robust, branched stems thickly covered with leaves that are elliptic-ovate to lanceolate in outline with serrate margins. The flower heads, up to 2.5 cm across, are arranged in dense corymbose panicles.

219

220

221

The tubular disc florets are bisexual, the ligulate ray florets female. The fruits are cylindrical with longitudinal ribs and gleaming whitish pappus. This plant is found in the temperate regions of Eurasia and North America, generally growing in greater numbers in woodland clearings, glades, damp open coniferous woods and thickets bordering streams from lowland to submontane elevations — in foothills often beside springs or in damp woodland margins.

Senecio haworthii (Haw.) Sch. Bip. (220) is a fleshy-leaved species of groundsel. Succulence is a rare condition amongst members of the composite family. The illustrated species is superbly adapted to the dry to semidesert conditions of its native environment — Africa's Cape Province. The plant reaches a height of 30 cm and has alternate, pointed, white-felted leaves and florets arranged in a large terminal head. It is grown as an ornamental.

Common Groundsel (221) differs at a glance from related species by its narrow, cylindrical,
Senecio vulgaris L. closed heads with glossy red-tipped involucral bracts. The heads are short-stalked and arranged in scanty terminal cymes. The tubular florets are pale yellow, the ray florets are absent. A characteristic feature of this species is that the heads droop after flowering and that they

222

224

flower in succession, so that a single plant may have both flowering and fruiting heads at the same time. The fruits are thickly covered with down and have a pure white shining pappus. Common Groundsel is a weed of field crops and is also found in places marked by man's activity, for instance burned ground, clearings, abandoned mining sites and waste places near cities.

Scentless Mayweed (222) unlike the related, aromatic chamomiles (genus *Matricaria*), is scent-less. The leaves are finely divided into thread-like segments. The stems are terminated by solitary heads up to 4 cm in diameter. The involucre is membranous on the edge. The tubular disc florets are golden-yellow, the ray florets are white and spreading at first, later drooping. As indi-cated by the Latin name *maritimum* this plant is often found in mari-time regions where its stems are prostrate. In Europe's hinterland it is common in semiruderal places and as a weed in cultivated fields where its stems are thick, erect and branched at the top. It is often found in grain crops, either on moist loamy-sandy soils or soils rich in nitrates.

Tripleurospermum
maritimum (L.) Koch

Pineapple Weed or Rayless Mayweed (223) is a strongly scented plant containing aromatic volatile oils. It differs from other chamomiles in that the heads are without ray florets. They are composed of a yellow-green disc of tubular florets supported by a hemispherical involucre consisting of bracts with translucent membranous margins. This chamomile is native

Matricaria discoidea
DC.

to North America; in Europe it occurs only as a naturalized species, even though it is often found in large numbers in widely diverse situations. It generally grows in grassy places, by waysides, in ditches and in sandy-loamy soil as a field weed. It is often encountered in nitrogen-rich soils. Though it has the typical aroma of chamomile it does not contain effective healing substances and is therefore not collected for medicinal purposes.

German Chamomile (224) has a pleasant, delicate aroma due to the volatile oils contained
Matricaria
chamomilla L.
chiefly in the heads. The stem leaves are pinnate, divided into thread-like segments; the flower heads are long-stalked and solitary, borne singly at the top of the stem, with recurved ray florets and hollow, conical receptacles. German Chamomile is a thermophilous species generally found in loamy sandy soils as a field weed in empty places or fallow land; however it is disappearing from its natural habitats due to the use of herbicides. Probably no other medicinal herb has won such widespread popularity as chamomile. Nowadays it is grown on a large scale as a very important, widely used drug. It is found in Eurasia, North America and Australia.

Common Dandelion (225) forms spreading masses in sunny grassy places in spring. It grows
Taraxacum
officinale Web.
practically everywhere, from lowland to foothill regions except in very wet places and woodlands. The deeply runcinate leaves are arranged in a basal rosette from which rises a hollow, erect flower stalk terminated

226

227

by a large head composed only of bisexual ligulate florets with a double row of involucral bracts beneath. The fruits which are ribbed are furnished with a fine pappus of toothed hairs. As the fruit matures the combined pappi jut from the receptacle to form the characteristic downy spheres known to all. The tissues of all the plant organs contain lactiferous ducts which ooze a milky sap when bruised.

British Fleabane (226) is found in Europe and Asia in diverse habitats for it has a great
Inula britannica L. ecological tolerance and can thus grow in varied conditions. It is found chiefly in damp meadows, on sunny grassy slopes and as a field weed mostly in light, loamy-sandy soils. The stem is branched and generally

221

228

covered with appressed hairs, as are the undersides of the elliptic leaves. The heads are hemispherical with silky-downy involucral bracts. The tubular disc florets and the very narrow ligulate ray florets are orange to golden-yellow. All species of fleabane are characterized by very narrow linear ray florets.

Irish Fleabane (227) also has heads of golden-yellow flowers but the involucral bracts are
Inula salicina L.   scarious. The stems are erect, unbranched, and densely covered with elongate, glossy, dark green leaves that are prominently veined on the underside, faintly toothed on the margins, shortly downy, and pointed at the tip. This species is common on shrubby sunny slopes and in stony, grassy hedgerows; it is also found in wet muddy meadows and inundated places alongside water courses.

Caucasian Leopardsbane (228) is a robust plant more than half a metre tall with stems sparsely
Doronicum   branched at the bottom and glandular-hairy. The basal leaves are large
caucasicum M. Bieb.   and deeply heart-shaped with broad winged stalks, the lower stem

leaves have short stalks clasping the stem, and the uppermost leaves are sessile, clasping the stem at the base, and deeply toothed on the margins. This leopardsbane is distributed in southeastern Europe and the Middle East but its large-flowered form, var. *magnificum,* is widely cultivated in European gardens.

Ligularia sibirica (L.) Cass. (229) is a robust plant up to 1.5 metre high. The stems are covered at the bottom with typical triangular leaves, heart-shaped at the base and sharply-toothed on the margins. They are terminated by heads of tubular disc florets and strap-shaped ray florets arranged in a dense raceme. This species is found only in bog and peat meadows and by flowing water from hilly country to piedmont areas. It is distributed in central and southeastern Europe eastward through the Caucasus to western Siberia. The genus *Ligularia* includes some twenty species distributed from western Europe to Japan. Many Asian species and hybrids are grown as ornamentals, chiefly for their robust stems and large leaves.

229

230

Great or Stemless Carline Thistle (230) is unusual in that it rarely develops a stem, which is usually completely atrophied, and the large, solitary head sits in the *Carlina acaulis* L. centre of the leaf rosette. The leaves are stiff, pale green and edged with spiny teeth of unequal length. The flower head measures up to 15 cm in diameter. The inner involucral bracts, resembling ray florets, are glossy white on the upper side and yellowish on the underside, conspicuously pointed and usually expanded. The disc florets, up to 2 cm long, are whitish but may also be pinkish. This Carline Thistle grows chiefly on dry slopes, in meadows and in grassy pasturelands but also in shrubby hedgerows and by forest margins. It is very tolerant in terms of altitude and is thus found from lowland to subalpine elevations. It is distributed throughout practically all of Europe and has many related species in the Mediterranean region and the Middle East. It was formerly cultivated for its high content of essential oils which were used to treat skin diseases and parasitoses; the young heads were used in salads.

Common Butterbur (231) grows on the banks of streams, in inundated meadows, damp wood-
Petasites hybridus   land margins, and beside springs from lowland to mountain districts. It
(L.) G. M. Sch.   flowers early in spring when the thick rhizome bears an erect stem
terminated by a dense raceme of many heads. The flowers are usually
pale to dark greyish-red, very occasionally white. The large, long-
stalked leaves appear after the flowers have faded. The stalk is up to
1 metre long and the broadly heart-shaped blade up to 60 cm wide; the
upper surface is randomly hairy and the underside greyish-woolly, particularly in new, developing leaves. The fruits are furnished with a long,
dingy white pappus which remains in evidence for a long time as the
stems gradually become longer. A striking characteristic of this plant is
the unpleasant odour that becomes more pronounced when the green
parts of the plant are rubbed between the fingers.

231

Giant Golden-rod (232) reaches a height of 2 metres and has a simple, erect stem thickly
Solidago gigantea covered with leaves at the bottom. The leaves are narrowed at both
Ait. ends, pointed at the tips, finely toothed on the margins and hairy on the undersides. The inflorescence is huge, terminal, pyramidal, and composed of one-sided racemes on arching stems. The racemes consist of solitary, short-stalked heads with several rows of involucral bracts. The tubular disc florets are golden-yellow as are the ray florets. The fruits are cylindrical with prominent longitudinal ribs and a simple rough pappus. Golden-rod is native to North America but is naturalized and common in Europe where it forms large masses, chiefly in shoreline thickets alongside water courses and also beside roads. It is grown as an ornamental in gardens, usually as a cross with other related American species of *Solidago*. The genus includes species native to both North and South America as well as to Europe and Asia. Some even grow in wet soil in upland pasturelands and in alpine grasslands beside water courses at mountain to subalpine elevations.

232

233

Tansy (233) is a tufted perennial more than 1 metre high with erect, thickly leaved stems terminated by dense inflorescences composed of small heads. The tubular disc florets are golden-yellow, the ray florets are absent or very short. Tansy is found in places often spoiled in some way — sometimes even in semiruderal places, on railway embankments, and alongside highways. It is also found in shoreline thickets alongside water courses and sometimes even in woodland glades and clearings from lowland to foothill regions throughout all Europe and Asia. Tansy was formerly used in folk medicine to eradicate intestinal parasites and promote digestion as it contains large amounts of essential oils and tannins. It has a long flowering period, throughout the whole summer until late autumn.

Tanacetum vulgare L. (syn. *Chrysanthemum vulgare* (L.) Bernh.)

227

235

Ox-eye Daisy (234) is found in the meadows of Europe and Asia at various altitudes and
Chrysanthemum   therefore in diverse environmental conditions, which is why it is ex-
leucanthemum L.   tremely variable within its range. The large terminal heads are composed of tubular disc florets and strap-shaped ray florets. The generic
name includes the word *chrysos,* meaning golden, which doubtless refers to the golden disc flowers. The genus *Chrysanthemum* embraces
a great many species whose large-flowered and double forms (derived
from east Asian species) are popular garden plants. They are among
the last of the flowering garden perennials, often bearing blossoms
until the frost in November and December.

Coneflower (235) is native to North America and is often grown in Europe's parks and gardens
Rudbeckia fulgida   for its showy heads. The stems, branched at the top, are up to 80 cm
Ait.   high and shortly hairy. The leaves are alternate, undivided, and shortly
pubescent, with three prominent veins and serrated margins. The tubular disc florets are bisexual and have a short corolla tube; the ray
florets are expanded but droop when they are spent and soon fall. The
fruits are prominently four-angled and are without a pappus.

Spear Thistle (236) grows on sunny shrubby slopes and in pastureland in relatively dry condi-
Cirsium vulgare
(Savi) Airy-Shaw
tions as well as in damp open woods and shoreline thickets alongside water courses from lowland to mountain districts. The stem is cobwebby and bristly, the leaves divided into ovate lobed segments terminating in thick pale yellow spines. All are covered with bristly hairs on the upper surface and with curly down on the underside. The solitary terminal head is composed of pale reddish-violet or white, pink-tinged flowers subtended by ovate involucral bracts with black-brown tips terminated by a yellow spine.

236

237

Cabbage Thistle (237) is a wetland species found in damp and inundated meadows, on the
Cirsium oleraceum banks of water courses and in damp roadside ditches in lowland and
(L.) Scop. hilly country. It is also encountered in mountain districts where it
grows beside springs and in valleys, its unusual yellow-green colour
making it a conspicuous element. It has a thick, glabrous stem more
then 1 metre high with soft, prickleless leaves edged with soft
spines and coloured fresh green. The heads are clustered at the tops of
the stems and the involucres are faintly cobwebby on the outside. The
flowers are yellowish-white, occasionally reddish. The Cabbage Thistle
readily interbreeds with related species, a characteristic feature of all
members of the genus *Cirsium*. Even triple hybrids, whose parentage
includes three different species, are not at all uncommon.

238

239

Cirsium canum (L.) All. (238) has erect, unbranched stems that are leafless and cobwebby in the upper half. The terminal heads are composed of a great many flowers up to 2 cm long. This thistle is found chiefly in damp meadows, wet woodlands, ditches and beside springs from lowland to foothill districts. It also readily interbreeds with related species in all its habitats.

Variegated Knapweed (239) grows on limestone, dolomite and volcanic rock substrates. It has *Centaurea triumfettii* a grey-felted, sparsely branched stem with soft, white downy leaves. All. The large heads have differently coloured disc and ray florets, and the involucres have fringed, toothed edges. The genus *Centaurea* includes several hundred small species distributed throughout the temperate regions of the northern hemisphere, usually distinguished by the shape and margin of the involucral bracts; the colour of the flowers also varies widely and may even be yellow or white.

Dahlia (240) is native to Mexico and, as the scientific name indicates, is a hybrid developed in *Dahlia × hybrida* cultivation. The great variability of the heads, particularly in the colour, hort. shape and length of the ligulate florets, has made these flowers great favourites of nurserymen. They include a wide variety of double forms, all of hybrid origin.

233

Spiny Thistle (241) with its robust habit, colour and large flower heads is a dominating element
Carduus acanthoides L. amidst the surrounding vegetation, and is even more striking when it occurs singly. The stems are up to 1 metre high, erect, much branched at the top and wavy-winged beneath the heads. The wings and leaf segments are spiny-lobed or spiny-toothed. The heads, composed of reddish-violet flowers, are borne singly at the ends of the branches. They remain on the plant until late summer. Spiny Thistle is usually found in pastureland, hedgerows and on shrubby slopes, also in waste places, fallow land, by waysides, and on road shoulders, chiefly in lowland and hilly country, for it is a thermophilous plant. The genus *Carduus* includes approximately 50 species distributed in Europe, Asia, northern Africa and the Canary Islands. All have very spiny stems and leaves and are therefore not usually grown as ornamentals. Related species of thistles readily interbreed. Hybrids are easily recognized, chiefly by the pink-tinged white flowers in the heads.

241

242

Great Globe-thistle (242) has robust, erect, angled stems up to 2 metres high, white pubescent
Echinops   to glandular-hairy at the top and simple or only sparsely branched. The
sphaerocephalus L.   stem leaves are long-stalked and pinnatifid with spiny-toothed segments. The globose terminal inflorescences, 4 to 8 cm in diameter, are
composed of a great many single-flowered heads. The flowers are grey
to steely blue and subtended by typical involucral bracts with fringed
ciliate margins. The fruits are covered with silky hairs and furnished
with a pappus fringed halfway to the base. This thistle is found in dry
grassy and stony places from lowland to foothill districts throughout
all the warm, temperate regions of Eurasia. Related species are often
grown as ornamentals not only for their attractive habit but also for
the beautifully coloured, pale violet to blue flowers of the globose
heads.

Chapter 9

GAMOPETALOUS PLANTS

This heterogeneous group includes many families of dicotyledonous plants which jointly give the vegetation of summer its distinctive aspect; they are all to a great degree similar, in terms of both ecological conditions of their natural habitats and their basic physiognomy.

In older botanical literature gamopetalous plants (ones that have petals united to form a tube) were often grouped together. From the modern phylogenetic viewpoint this grouping is in great measure unacceptable for the evolution of vascular plants followed more complicated paths and this gamopetalous condition is found in many distantly related families.

Toadflax (243) has a thick stem nearly 1 metre high thickly covered with linear, alternate
Linaria vulgaris Mill.　leaves. The flowers are stalked and arranged at the tops of the stems in conical racemes. The bilabiate corolla has a two-lobed upper lip, a three-lobed lower lip and a hollow spur. Toadflax is found in grassy hedgerows, at the edges of field crops, in pasturelands and in woodland clearings. It is often a pioneer plant in new, as yet barren places, such as embankments and dikes. It is distributed throughout all Europe from the British Isles to the Urals, including the Mediterranean region and the Caucasus; in the north, in Scandinavia, it extends beyond the Arctic Circle. In Asia it extends to Lake Baikal and has become naturalized in all North America; on the Pacific coast it grows south of the equator to Chile.

Curl-leafed Mint (244) is a curl-leafed garden species obtained by crossbreeding. Besides the
Mentha spicata L.　unusual deeply divided leaves it is noteworthy for its variability in the
em. Huds. var. *crispa*　size of the spike-like inflorescence and in the colouration of the flowers.
Danert　The illustrated cultivar is usually classed together with the type species

244

— Spearmint or Common Green Mint — which like most mints grows in damp shoreline thickets, ditches and often as a field weed in damp loamy-sandy soils. It is distributed from lowland to foothill districts throughout the temperate regions of Eurasia.

Horse Mint (245) is a robust perennial with stems grey-felted their entire length and a large spike-like inflorescence. The terminal spikes are composed of violet-red flowers and are very striking in the shoreline thickets, beside watercourses and in the damp ditches where they grow. Often grown in gardens is the curly-leafed form *undulata.*

Mentha longifolia
(L.) Huds.

Corn Mint (246) is very tolerant in terms of ecological conditions and is found in wet ground as well as in soil with a tendency to dry out, occurring most commonly as a weed of field crops and on fallow land, sometimes also in meadow communities. The stem, often violet, is covered with spreading hairs and stalked leaves that are ovate in outline and shallowly serrate on the margins. The flowers grow from the upper leaf axils and are clustered in cylindrical spikes. The calyx is bell-shaped or trumpet-shaped and the lilac corolla tube is terminated by four lobes, the upper two

Mentha arvensis L.

245

246

247

joined to form a lip. Corn Mint readily interbreeds with related species
of *Mentha* and also figures in the parentage of hybrids that are grown
as ornamentals, chiefly various curl-leafed forms; they often become
naturalized. Corn Mint has a continuous distribution extending from
Great Britain to Lake Baikal; it is also found in central Asia and India,
Japan, the Philippines, New Zealand and North America.

Flesh-coloured Heath (247) is noted for its flesh-coloured flowers arranged in dense terminal
Erica herbacea L. racemes. It grows in dry pinewoods, chiefly on basic rock substrates. It
is distributed in central Europe — in the northern and southern perialpine regions — whence it extends to northern Italy and the western
part of the Balkan Peninsula.

Garden Sage (248) is a strongly aromatic plant with very stiff, persistent leaves that are finely
Salvia officinalis L.   crenate on the margin. The young stems are woolly, becoming woody
at the base in time. Sage is found in sunny rocky situations in Europe's
Mediterranean region and is often grown in gardens for its high content of aromatic volatile oils. The leaves of this species are used as
a component of herbal tea mixtures.

Tuberous Comfrey (249) is a perennial plant with erect, unbranched stems covered with
Symphytum   spreading hairs along their entire length. The leaves are all nearly ses-
tuberosum L.   sile, heart-shaped in outline with entire margins and pronounced veins
on the underside. The stems are terminated by drooping inflorescences
of short-stalked pendulous flowers subtended by bracts. A closer look
at the funnel-shaped corolla reveals small conical outgrowths or forni-

248

249

ces in the throat (probably remnants of a second row of stamens) arranged alternately with five stamens in a single row. The fruits are composed of five sections and have a tubercled surface. This species is found in damp leafy woods, wet alder groves, floodplain forests and damp meadows from lowland to foothill districts. Its distribution in Europe extends from central Spain and central France to the region bordering the Black Sea; it is often a component of the flora of central and southeastern Europe and is also encountered in the British Isles.

Common Comfrey (250), as the scientific name *officinale* indicates, was commonly used in folk
Symphytum medicine, chiefly in medieval days, for the essential oils and tannins it
officinale L. contains. The turnip-like root, coloured black outside and white inside, bears a bristly-hairy stem covered with alternate, rough, hairy leaves. The dense drooping inflorescences are composed of short-stalked flowers each with a tubular-urceolate corolla coloured dingy reddish-violet, occasionally yellowish-white. This plant is found throughout all Eurasia to western Siberia.

250

Wrinklenut (251) has stems covered with greyish-white felt consisting of bristly and glandular
Nonea pulla (L.) DC. hairs. The leaves, arranged in a ground rosette, are also covered with
prominent hairs. The short-stalked flowers grow from the upper leaf
axils and have a tubular-funnel-shaped corolla coloured brownish-vio-
let, pinkish-white or yellowish. This species is found in dry meadows,
pastureland, hedgerows and along roadsides, chiefly at lower elevations. It has a continuous distribution from central Europe throughout
the temperate regions of Eurasia to western Siberia, including the
Black Sea region, and it also grows in scattered localities throughout
western Europe.

Viper's Bugloss (252) has stout stems more than 1 metre high, which, together with the leaves,
Echium vulgare L. are covered with spreading bristly hairs growing from minute warts.
The flowers, in dense cylindrical inflorescences, grow from the upper
leaf axils. The funnel-shaped, bilabiate corolla is coloured pink when it
opens and is usually blue in full bloom. Viper's Bugloss is found chiefly
in grassy hedgerows, on slopes by waysides, on railway embankments
and even in semiruderal situations such as the edges of fields. It is
a Eurasian species distributed from the British Isles to central Siberia
and extending northward to central Scandinavia.

242

251

252

254

Spiked Speedwell (253) is a very variable species particularly as regards the hairs of the stems.
Veronica spicata L. Topping the stems are racemose inflorescences up to 30 cm long, composed of stalked, tubular funnel-shaped flowers that open in succession from the bottom upward. Spiked Speedwell grows on sunny grassy slopes and in open leafy groves, chiefly on basic rock substrates. Its distribution is centred in the southern regions of Europe where it occurs as several subspecies.

Agapetes serpens Sleum. (254) has branches that are usually glandular-pubescent in youth and
(syn. *Pentapterygium* covered with alternate shining leaves; they become woody with age.
serpens Klotzsch) The flowers, generally paired, have short hairy stalks and a prominent urceolate corolla with a toothed edge. This species is found in India, Nepal and Sikkim below the Himalayas at elevations between 1,000 and 2,500 metres, where there is ample precipitation during the growth period and where coniferous forests of pine and cedar predominate.

Thyme (255) has a prostrate, four-angled stem covered with short hairs and opposite, glandular leaves. The flowers are clustered in dense terminal spikes and grow from the axils of the upper leaves. All the aerial parts contain strongly aromatic volatile oils, which particularly on hot summer days give off a penetrating, pleasant scent. This species forms dense cushions in dry sunny situations where it occurs in spreading masses. It is found in the mountain meadows of central Europe, in the Pannonian range, High Sudetens and through the western Carpathians to the southern Carpathians. Species of thyme readily interbreed in the wild and the parentage of the hybrids is very difficult to determine. Thymes were widely used in folk medicine and are still used as components in many medicinal preparations.

Thymus alpestris
Tausch

255

256

Cut-leaved Self-heal (256) was so named for its laciniate leaves, cut deeply into narrow jagged
Prunella laciniata L. segments. The flowers, arranged in cylindrical spikes at the tops of the
stems, have a two-lipped calyx and tubular, two-lipped corolla. Both
labiate corolla lobes are yellowish-white which is something of an exception amongst members of the genus *Prunella,* most of which are
coloured bluish-violet. This plant is a thermophilous species generally
found on grassy, stony slopes and in dry semi-steppe meadows. It is
distributed from the Iberian Peninsula through central and southern
Europe to north Africa and through the Caucasus to the Caspian Sea.

247

257

Large-flowered Self-heal (257) is noted for its large capitate racemes of bluish-violet flow-
Prunella grandiflora ers growing from the axils of heart-shaped, pointed bracts. Typical
(L.) Jacq. features of the flowers are the two-lipped calyx and tubular corolla.
This plant grows on sunny, semi-steppe slopes, being partial to lime-
stone rather than volcanic rock substrates. It is distributed in Europe
from the Pyrenees to the central Urals, including the Black Sea region
and Ciscaucasia, and extends northward to Denmark and southern
Sweden.

248

Melittis melissophyllum L. (258) has the green aerial parts permeated with aromatic volatile oils which emit a strong, penetrating scent, particularly in full sunlight in dry situations. The stem is covered with soft spreading hairs with one-sided whorls of large, long-stalked, prominently labiate flowers growing from the axils of the upper leaves. Because this is a thermophilous species it is generally encountered in lowland and hill country in thin, sun-dappled broad-leaved woods and amidst shrubs on stony, grassy slopes. It is distributed throughout all southern and central Europe and occurs sporadically in the western Ukraine, northern Poland, Germany and southeastern England.

Spotted Dead-nettle (259) has a prominently four-angled, simple stem coloured violet and *Lamium maculatum* L. covered with long-stalked leaves. The whorled inflorescences in the uppermost leaf axils are composed of sessile, rose-red flowers. Spotted Dead-nettle is found in widely diverse habitats — from open woodlands and shrubby slopes to roadside ditches and waysides — and often occurs as a weed in fields and gardens.

258

259

260

White Dead-nettle (260), like the preceding species, has flowers arranged in terminal whorls in the
Lamium album L. uppermost leaf axils. They are sessile and coloured white or with a faint yellowish hue. The whole stem is covered with downy hairs and the lower half is coloured violet. This species has a continuous distribution from the British Isles to central Siberia and is also found throughout the arctic regions of the USSR. In the south it extends to Iran and has been introduced to Iceland and North America.

Large Hemp-nettle (261) is a plant of shrubby, shaded woodland margins as well as glades and
Galeopsis speciosa woodland clearings. It is often found in places affected by man's activi-
Mill. ty, for instance woodland clearings or burnt areas. The whole stem is covered with spreading bristly hairs and is inflated beneath the nodes where it branches. The leaves are long-stalked and ovate with serrate margins and prominent veins. The flowers are arranged in many-flow-ered terminal whorls growing from the upper leaf axils; the corolla tube is yellowish-white and the two lips sulphur-yellow with purple markings at the base of the lower lip. Some hemp-nettles, including the Large Hemp-nettle, readily interbreed. The flowers of the hybrids are intermediate in shade between those of the parent species. Large Hemp-nettle is distributed from Great Britain throughout all northern and central Europe to the Balkan Peninsula in the southeast and north-ward to the Arctic Circle. In Asia it is distributed throughout all west-ern Siberia to the upper reaches of the Yenisei River.

261

262

Ground Ivy (262) has branched, prostrate or ascending stems covered with random hairs. The *Glechoma hederacea* L. leaves are stalked and kidney-shaped with crenate margins. The flowers are relatively large and grow from the axils of the middle and upper leaves; the bilabiate corolla is thinly hairy, the upper lip two-lobed and the lower lip large and three-lobed. Ground Ivy is a photophilic plant found on grassy slopes, in meadows, at forest margins and in shrubby hedgerows throughout all Eurasia from the British Isles to Lake Baikal, primarily in temperate and northern regions, extending occasionally beyond the Arctic Circle. It has also been introduced to the United States.

252

Wood Betony (263) has long-stalked basal leaves with shallowly heart-shaped bases and coarsely
Betonica officinalis crenate margins; they are glabrous above and hairy on the undersur-
L. (syn. *Stachys* face. The flowers are subtended by small bracts and arranged in dense
officinalis L.) terminal cylindrical spikes. The corolla tube is slightly curved; the
middle lobe of the lower lip is large and crenate whereas the upper lip
is erect and hairy. This plant is found in dry meadows, open broad-
leaved woods and clearings from lowland to foothill districts.

263

Upright Bugle (264) has erect, thickly glandular-hairy stems, a rosette of basal leaves and
Ajuga genevensis L. short-stalked stem leaves. The flowers, subtended by insignificant
three-lobed bracts, are arranged in a terminal spike-like inflorescence.
The calyx is bell-shaped, the corolla tubular and labiate and coloured
violet-blue, occasionally pink to white. Bugle is a thermophilous plant
partial to dry open places, open groves and scrub throughout all Europe. It is distributed from the Pyrenees to the central Urals including
the Balkan Peninsula and western Caucasus and also extends north to
Scandinavia, where it was introduced. It often interbreeds with other
related species of *Ajuga*.

Common Motherwort (265) is a plant of dry pastureland and waste places and the scientific
Leonurus cardiaca L. name *cardiaca* indicates the useful properties it possesses. In folk medicine it was known that the tannins and essential oils of motherwort
stimulated heart activity. The plant has a richly branched stem covered
with spreading hairs and stalked, heart-shaped leaves. The flowers are
sessile and arranged in dense whorls in the axils of the middle and
upper leaves. The corolla is pinkish or whitish and woolly, the lower lip
divided into brown-coloured lobes.

Wild or Pot Marjoram, Oregano (266) has a very pleasant, thyme-like fragrance (it contains
Origanum vulgare L. thymol as does thyme). It, too, is a herb that provides food for bees and
was used as a kitchen herb for its high concentration of essential oils
and tannins; it also has strong disinfectant properties. The stems are ter-

264

265

266

minated by dichasial inflorescences in which even the bracts are violet.
The corolla tube is pale red to dingy white, the lower lip three-lobed,
the upper lip shallowly notched. This species is distributed from Great
Britain throughout the temperate and southern regions of Europe; in
Asia its range extends north to Lake Baikal and south from the Cauca-
sus through the Pamir region to Kashmir. The closely related Sweet
Marjoram *(O. majorana* L.*)* is grown for its aromatic leaves which are
used in cooking.

Wild or Fuller's Teasel (267) is a remarkably robust plant with an angular stem more than
Dipsacus sylvestris 2 metres high that has spines on the angles and which branches by
Huds. forking at the top. The basal leaves, arranged in a rosette, are short-
stalked and elliptic with crenate margins and prickly upper surfaces.
The stem leaves, joined at the base into pairs, are entire with spines
along the margins and on the median ribs of the underside. The most

267

striking feature is the dense cylindrical inflorescence at the top of each stem composed of prickly linear bracts subtending the individual flowers. The latter have a tubular funnel-shaped corolla more than 1 cm long and open in succession from the centre of the inflorescence outward. This teasel is distributed in the temperate and southern regions of Europe where it occurs in places that are usually without a contiguous cover of vegetation, for instance ditches alongside highways, banks of water courses, railway embankments and semiruderal situations. Some related species are grown as ornamentals and dried for winter decoration.

Carpathian Bellflower
Campanula carpatica Jacq.
(268) has a sparsely branched stem, usually thinly hairy, with stalked, heart-shaped, pointed leaves that are shining on the upper side. The loose terminal raceme is composed of long-stalked flowers that straighten when they open so that the corolla is broadly bell-shaped, up to 4 cm long and divided for about a quarter of its length into wide pointed lobes. The narrowly lanceolate sepals are outspread after the

flowers have faded. This bellflower forms thick clumps, the colouration of the leaves and flowers making them a striking feature from afar.

Clustered Bellflower (269) has flowers arranged in whorled, many-flowered clusters. The corolla is bell-shaped and coloured violet, very occasionally white. A striking characteristic of this species is the difference in the leaves — the basal leaves are long-stalked and elliptic, the stem leaves short-stalked to sessile. This bellflower has a broad vertical distribution. It is found in both lowland and mountain districts, often above the forest limit, mostly in open grassy places.

Campanula glomerata L.

Spreading Bellflower (270) has erect stems more than 50 cm high with sessile elliptic leaves. The basal leaves are rounded ovate and short-stalked. The flowers are long-stalked and arranged in loose branched racemes at the tops of the stems. The calyx has long lobes about half the length of the funnel-shaped corolla, which is deeply divided into pointed lobes coloured pale

Campanula patula L.

268

269

270

271

to dark blue, very occasionally white. Even though all bellflowers typically have violet-blue petals, each species also produces white-flowered individuals that are otherwise no different from the rest. This property is particularly welcomed by nurserymen and makes the populations of the respective species more colourful and varied. Spreading Bellflower is a Eurasian species that is very variable, mainly in relation to elevation — lowland populations differ from those found in mountains and are usually classed as separate subspecies. It grows chiefly in dry meadows, hedgerows, glades and open woodland clearings. Species of *Campanula* tend to prefer dry situations — they are found less often in damp environments.

Yellow Foxglove (271)
Digitalis grandiflora
Mill.

is a striking plant with erect, robust, glandular pubescent stem and alternate, longish-lanceolate leaves, shallowly serrate on the margins. The flowers, arranged in one-sided racemes, are short-stalked and drooping; the tubular bell-shaped corolla has a broad lobed rim and is coloured pale ochre with brown spots within and covered with glandular down outside. This species is found in grassy places in mixed woods and in woodland margins and clearings often extending from lowland and hilly districts to spreads of dwarf pine in mountain districts. In Europe it has a continuous distribution from France to the central Ukraine, through the Balkans to Greece and in the north to the Baltic countries; in the central Urals and western Siberia it is sporadic and local in occurrence.

273

Purple Foxglove (272) also has a robust stem with long-stalked ovate leaves. The stalked
Digitalis purpurea L. flowers, clustered in dense one-sided racemes, open in succession from
the bottom upward. The calyx is shortly bell-shaped whereas the corolla is broadly funnel-shaped. This plant is distributed throughout Europe, being found chiefly in woodland glades, margins and clearings in mixed and coniferous woods in foothill and mountain districts. In some regions it has become a popular ornamental and often grows as an escape near mountain gardens. Nowadays the drug obtained from foxgloves, chiefly from *Digitalis lanata* Ehrh., is one of the most effective of cardiac medicines.

Water Forget-me-not (273) has characteristic, delicate, blue flowers arranged in a corymbose
Myosotis palustris inflorescence. The stem and leaves are often very fragile and brittle.
(L.) Nath. This species grows chiefly in damp situations, ones that are shaded

rather than sunny, and is common alongside streams, ponds and in damp meadows; in mountain districts it is found primarily by water courses, mountain streams and springs. It is distributed throughout all Europe excepting the Iberian Peninsula, extending through the Urals to western and central Siberia as far as Lake Baikal. In the north it extends almost to 70° North. It exhibits marked variability throughout its range.

Dracocephalum austriacum L. (274) is a rare thermophilous plant found in Europe from eastern France to the western Ukraine. The erect, sparsely branched stem is woolly along the entire length and the leaves are divided into linear, pointed segments. The flowers, clustered in terminal whorls subtended by bracts, are strikingly large and coloured deep bluish-violet, occasionally pink or white. The corolla is up to 4 cm long with a very long, spreading tube, erect upper lip and curving lower lip.

274

275

276

Phlox setacea L. (275) is often grown in gardens in many differently coloured forms. It has erect, branched stems and flowers clustered in terminal cymose inflorescences. The tubular corollas with spreading lobes are generally white, pink or violet. This plant is native to North America.

Common Figwort (276) contains unpleasantly smelling substances, the odour being most pro-
Scrophularia nodosa L. nounced when the foliage is crushed, and thus is not a popular herb. The stems are four-angled, unbranched and covered with opposite, short-stalked leaves. The flowers, arranged in loose, terminal spikes, are long-stalked with a broad bell-shaped calyx and a corolla consisting of an inflated tube and two short brownish-red lips. This species grows in shoreline thickets, shrubby hedgerows and in damp riverine woods. It is distributed from the British Isles to the upper reaches of the Yenisei River in central Siberia and in Europe extends along the Norwegian coast beyond the Arctic Circle.

White Mullein (277) grows on sunny, grassy and stony slopes, in pastureland, screes, and open
Verbascum lychnitis L. groves but is also found in abandoned quarries as well as on railway embankments and highway verges. It is of robust habit with stem often 1.5 metres high. The latter is erect, branched in panicle-like fashion at the top and finely felted along its entire length. The basal leaves are

263

short-stalked, ovate and sinuate-crenate on the margin, the stem leaves sessile and elliptic; both are glabrous above, green and thickly white-felted on the underside. The flowers, arranged in dense pyramidal inflorescences, are up to 2 cm across and have white-woolly filaments.

Large-flowered Mullein (278) reaches a height of approximately 2 metres. The stem is thickly hairy with alternate, softly felted leaves that become smaller towards the top of the stem. The flowers are arranged in terminal racemes and measure up to 5 cm in diameter. This species is found throughout all Europe in more or less the same situations as *V. lychnitis* (Fig. 277).

Verbascum thapsiforme Schrad. (syn. *Verbascum densiflorum* Bertol.)

Common Mullein (279) is a biennial with a robust stem, covered with a yellowish-white felt. The basal leaves are arranged in a rosette, the stem leaves are alternate. Both are felted and thus very soft. The flowers, in terminal racemes, have a pale yellow, funnel-shaped corolla up to 2 cm in diameter with typical white-woolly filaments. Common Mullein is found on sunny, stony slopes, in pastureland and in woodland glades, also in abandoned places, quarries, ditches and embankments. In all these situations it interbreeds with related species of mullein. The hybrids differ from the parent plants by the shape of the leaves and colour of the stamens.

Verbascum thapsus L.

277

278

Field Bindweed (280) has a prostrate or twining stem and long-stalked sagittate leaves. The *Convolvulus arvensis* L. relatively large solitary flower has a broadly funnel-shaped corolla, lobed at the edge and coloured white or tinted pink. Bindweed occurs as a weed in fields and gardens and otherwise grows in pastures, fallow land, by waysides and on rather dry grassy slopes. It is distributed throughout all North America, Europe and Asia and is also found in the southern hemisphere — in Argentina and Australia — where it was introduced.

Great Bindweed (281), like the preceding species, is a twining plant with branched stems and *Calystegia sepium* (L.) R. Br. large, long-stalked flowers. The funnel-shaped corolla is white or tinted pink and may be up to 6 cm long. This species generally spreads in damp thickets alongside water courses and in inundated riverine woods. In Europe it occurs chiefly in the western, central and southern regions, it is found in northern Africa and from Asia Minor to central Siberia; it is also a component of the flora of the Americas, where it grows in Chile, Argentina, on the Pacific coast of North America and by the Gulf of Mexico. It is also found in Australia and Japan.

279

Chapter 10   STRIKING AND ATTRACTIVE MONOCOTS

Monocotyledons are a natural group of plants which differ from dicotyledons in several ways. Their embryos, as the name of the group indicates, have only one cotyledon or seed-leaf. The radicle disappears soon after germination and is replaced by numerous adventitious roots. The leaves are usually narrow, linear in outline with entire margins and parallel venation. Only in certain members of the lily family are they broader and net-veined. The flowers are rarely solitary — as a rule they are arranged in very complex inflorescences; sometimes the entire inflorescence is subtended by a single bract called a spathe. The floral parts are generally in threes or multiples of three (in dicotyledons generally in fours or fives). They are usually not differentiated into a calyx and corolla and the perianth is often one colour. The pollen of monocotyledons has a more primitive structure and is more uniform in shape and size than that of dicotyledons.

Monocotyledons have become adapted to a variety of environments. For instance in the dry soil of steppes and arid regions they form bulbs or tuberous rhizomes, in the wet ground of poolsides and bogs they form rhizomes or tubers. In the tropical rain forests they occur as epiphytes attached to trees or other plants by means of aerial roots. In semiarid regions some species are able to absorb atmospheric moisture through special epidermal structures and pass it on to the leaf and stem tissues.

Monocotyledons include about 54,000 species, which is approximately a quarter of all flowering plants. The remainder are dicotyledons.

Aechmea chantinii (Carr.) Baker (282) has long, strap-shaped, horizontally striped leaves that form a striking contrast to the coloured bracts. The latter are broadly lanceolate with toothed margins and grow out and away from the stem at the base of the terminal, loosely branched spikes. This plant is found

283

in the tropical rain forests of the Amazon region. Without doubt one of the most attractive of the bromeliads, it grows as an epiphyte on the trunks of certain woody plants. The genus *Aechmea* embraces a great many species distributed from Mexico to Argentina.

Vallota purpurea (Ait.) Herb. (283) is a perennial with underground bulbs bearing long flower stalks with basal leaves and large, solitary, terminal flowers. It is a very attractive plant, native to Cape Province in South Africa, and often grown as an ornamental for room decoration.

Aloë × winteri Berger (284) is a cross between *A. salmdyckiana* and *A. arborescens,* both native to Cape Province in South Africa. It is not without interest that *A. arborescens* was one of the first aloës to be discovered and described. Its distinctive features include robust leaves up to 60 cm long· and lovely red tubular flowers. The second parent, *A. salmdyckiana,* has a stem up to 3 metres high and a huge basal rosette of stiff leaves up to 75 cm long. The hybrid is noted for its inflorescence — a raceme up to 25 cm long composed of red flowers approximately 3.5 cm long. Crossbreeding of *Aloë* species produces hybrids with larger and more colourful flowers.

284

285

286

287

Partridge-breasted Aloë or Tiger Aloë (285) attains a height of only 30 cm. The leaves, unlike
Aloë variegata L. those of most aloës, are arranged spirally in three rows at the bottom
of the stem. They are triangular, channelled on the inside, sharply
keeled on the outside, and coloured dark green with white markings on
the outer surface. The flowers with red, relatively long corolla lobes
are arranged in a terminal raceme. This species is native to Cape Province and has been a popular house plant since the early 18th century,
chiefly because of its attractive variegated foliage. Crossing with certain related species has produced a great many beautiful hybrids noted
for their striking leaf markings and the colouration of their flowers.

Aloë (286) is a hybrid obtained in cultivation. Its habit of growth and leaves indicate that one of
Aloë × hybrida hort. the parent species is *A. variegata,* but the other cannot definitely be
identified. Plants of the genus *Aloë,* numbering some 250 species, are
native to the semiarid regions of South Africa and are also found on
neighbouring islands in the Indian Ocean — in Madagascar, the Masca-
rene Islands and Socotra. They were introduced to Europe in about
1700 and since that time have been widely grown in subtropical greenhouses. They have a fleshy root and a stout stem several decimetres

272

high that becomes woody in time. Characteristic are the fleshy, sword-shaped leaves edged with spiny teeth and arranged in a basal rosette or forming a prominent crest at the top of the stem. The flowers are tubular, the fruit is a capsule. Some South African species of *Aloë* have special cells in the stem and leaf tissues that secrete a bitter juice which has eminent healing properties and which has been used in folk medicine since medieval time. The oxidized juice from crushed leaves formed a crumbly substance with purgative effects which could also be used in the preparation of dyes.

Cushion Aloë (287) grows wild in the semidesert regions of South Africa. The leaves are up to
Aloë sguarrosa 20 cm long and either sticky-felted or entirely glabrous. The species
Bak et Balf. occurs in many varieties differing in the consistency of the leaves.

289

Bulbine latifolia Roem. et Schult. (288) is likewise native to the semiarid regions of Cape Province in South Africa. The leafless flower stalk grows from a ground rosette of long, stiff, pointed leaves, measuring up to 7 cm in width in the lower half. The terminal raceme, up to 60 cm long, is composed of a great many small flowers that open in succession from the bottom upward. Certain related species of *Bulbine* are found in eastern Australia.

Ornithogalum orthophyllum Ten. (289) has an ovoid underground bulb without offsets from subsp. *kochii* (Parl.) which rises an erect flower stalk with narrowly linear, grey-green Zahar. leaves. The terminal corymb is composed of as many as twelve flowers on oblique stalks. The white perianth segments are elliptic, up to 2.5 cm long and expanded; the outer segments are usually wider than the inner segments. The fruit is a capsule that is faintly flattened with two prominent ridges at the top; the seeds are black and wrinkled. This plant is found on grassy slopes and in open woods in the lowland and hilly

290

country of central and southern Europe. It is not taxonomically uniform and occurs as several subspecies throughout its range. Members of the genus *Ornithogalum* are found chiefly in the drier and warm temperate regions of Europe and Asia; only a few grow in Cape Province. North America is the home of the closely related genus *Camassia.*

Ornithogalum nutans L. (290, 291) has an underground bulb with many offsets, by means of which it spreads. The grey-green leaves, arranged in a ground rosette, are linear and channelled and usually longer than the flowering stem. The flowers are persistent, subtended by membranous bracts and arranged in a terminal raceme (usually one-sided) or corymb. They are quite large (up to 5 cm in diameter) with stalks shorter than the flowers and drooping like bells. The perianth segments are white with a green stripe on the outside. Being a thermophilous species this ornithogalum grows in riverine woods and sandy fallow land and often as a weed in

291

292

293

vineyards. It is distributed in central and southeastern Europe to the Middle East. Like the preceding species it occurs as several subspecies throughout its range, differing in the shape of the filaments and anthers.

Ornithogalum pyramidale L. (292) has stems more than a metre high terminated by a pyramidal raceme composed of a great many flowers. The perianth segments are conspicuously longitudinally veined and curl when the flowers are spent. This plant is thermophilous and is found in fallow land, by waysides and sometimes also in fields amidst grain. It occurs in Europe as several subspecies differing in the length of the flower stalks.

Vriesea fenestralis Lind. et André (293) is an epiphytic species of the tropical rain forests of Brazil. The leaves, almost 50 cm long, about 8 cm wide and long-pointed, are arranged in a large funnel-shaped rosette. They are marked with a network pattern on the upper side and with large blotches on the undersurface. The flowering stem is about one metre high. The blooms are arranged in a loose spike with prominent bracts. The corolla lobes are not joined and have a peculiar appendage called a ligule inside at the base — its importance or function is not known. The genus *Vriesea* Lindl. includes approximately 180 species distributed in the tropical regions of Brazil. All require high atmospheric mois-

277

294

ture, high temperatures and shade. They are distributed great distances by means of the seeds which are furnished with 'parachutes' — a common feature of bromeliads.

May Lily (294) can be identified when not in flower by the broadly ovate leaves, each with *Maianthemum bifolium* (L.) F.W. Schmidt a heart-shaped base. It has a thin, creeping rhizome from which rises an erect, randomly pubescent stem with two, occasionally one or three, leaves. These are short-stalked, prominently veined and downy on the underside. The inflorescence is a raceme composed of two- or three-flowered umbels. The flowers, white or yellowish and fragrant, grow on short stalks from the axils of membranous bracts. The fruit is a bright cherry-red berry. May Lily grows in shaded, mossy, coniferous woods, in damp ravines by woodland streams and in broad-leaved woods from lowland to practically subalpine elevations throughout all Eurasia. North America is the home of the related species *M. cana-dense* Desf. The May Lily has a broad ecological tolerance, evident chiefly in its vertical distribution. It occurs in greater numbers in its natural habitats but non-flowering specimens always predominate.

Angular Solomon's Seal (295) has angled, arching stems with solitary flowers on stalks in the
Polygonatum
odoratum (Mill.)
Druce
axils of the leaves. It is a Eurasian species and is found primarily in thermophilic broad-leaved and pine woods and on stony and shrubby slopes, preferring basic rock substrates, such as limestone, dolomite and other volcanic rocks.

295

Heliconia bihai L. (296) reaches a height of more than 6 m and its huge inflorescence, 60 cm long and 30 cm wide, is composed of beautifully coloured flowers and equally attractive bracts. It is found in the tropical and subtropical regions of Central and South America.

Beardless or Siberian Iris (297) has a tall erect stem sparsely branched at the top. The leaves *Iris sibirica* L. are narrow and sword-shaped and almost never taller than the stems bearing one, two or three faintly scented flowers. This iris has a continuous distribution from the Rhine region throughout all central Europe, extending through the Ukraine and Urals almost to the upper Yenisei River; it grows scattered also in southeastern Europe, Turkey and Transcaucasia. It is a damp-loving plant and thus is found in wet grassy meadows and damp woodland margins. It is without doubt a lovely wild iris.

296

297

Iris pumila L. (298) is a tufted species with a very short stem growing from a creeping tuberous rhizome. The sword-shaped leaves are grey-green with prickly tips and they become longer after the flowers have faded. The flowers are sessile and enclosed at the base by two membranous bracts; the perianth segments are joined at the base to form a tube and divided at the top into three upright inner lobes and three recurved outer lobes. The entire perianth is longish-ovate and coloured violet, occasionally pink or yellow. A characteristic feature is the style terminated by three leaf-like, two-lipped stigma lobes. This iris is found on sunny stony slopes and in partially sandy, mainly calcareous loess soils. Its blooms wilt rapidly after flowering. It is distributed from central Europe east to the middle Volga region, including the Balkan Peninsula, Crimea and the Caucasus.

Alocasia indica (Roxb.) Schott (299) is called 'Tropical Indian Root' in tropical Asia for a distinguishing feature of the approximately 50 species of *Alocasia* are the starchy rhizomatous tubers. All these plants are native to Indomalaysia and are distributed chiefly in southeast Asia. The illustrated species is noted for its huge decorative leaves with blades up to 100 cm long.

298

299

Also attractive is the 15- to 20-cm-long spadix composed of small, yellow, bisexual flowers and enclosed by a white spathe. Most species are starch-producing plants but first and foremost they are handsome ornamentals grown in tropical greenhouses.

Guzmania monostachya (L.) Rusby (300) has a leaf rosette up to 40 cm across composed of pale green strap-shaped leaves up to 2.5 cm wide. From the centre of this rosette grows a stem nearly 50 cm high terminated by a dense spike-like inflorescence. The individual flowers are subtended by bracts that differ in colour depending on whether they are at the bottom or top of the spike. This plant, distributed from Florida through

300

Central America to Bolivia, is found chiefly in tropical rain forests with high atmospheric moisture. The evolutionary focus of the genus *Guzmania* is the tropical northwestern part of South America whence the separate species spread north and south.

Guzmania zahnii (Hook. fil.) Mez (301) has a basal rosette of soft leaves up to 60 cm long with prominent longitudinal veins on the upper side. The stem is very tall, the upper half covered with overlapping bracts. These are coloured, their effect being heightened by the flowers, up to 3 cm long, that are concealed by the bracts at first. The corolla lobes are joined to form a tube. This species is found in the damp tropical forests of Costa Rica and like all species of *Guzmania* has seeds furnished with striking 'parachutes' that contribute to its rapid dispersal.

Guzmania sanguinea (André) André (302) grows in the tropical rain forests of Central America and is distinguished by a flat funnel-shaped rosette composed of strap-shaped leaves up to 25 cm long and 4 to 5 cm wide. The inner leaves change colour during the flowering period. The inflorescence is a simple, many-flowered spike set deep inside the leaf funnel.

284

301

302

303

Herb Paris (303) has an erect stem terminated by a whorl of four (occasionally three to seven)
Paris quadrifolia L. leaves. From the centre of the whorl grows a long-stalked, 4-merous
flower with spreading segments; the outer perianth segments are up to
3 cm long, the inner segments slightly more than half that length. There
is a conspicuously awl-shaped connective joining the pollen sacs. The
fruit is a globose, blue-black, very poisonous berry. Herb Paris is found
primarily in broad-leaved woods and open mixed woods throughout
the temperate and northern regions of Europe and Asia. It has a continuous distribution from Great Britain to eastern Siberia; it is also found
in Iceland and in Scandinavia it extends along the Norwegian coast
beyond the Arctic Circle.

Crown Imperial (304, 305) has stems with glossy, lanceolate leaves positioned alternately at the
Fritillaria imperialis L. bottom, clustered densely in the middle and arranged in whorls at the top. The cluster of hanging, bell-like flowers is topped by a crest of green leaves. The flowers are orange to brick-red and have large, white, cup-shaped nectaries at the inside base of the perianth segments. The fruit is a six-angled, short-stalked capsule. This species, native to Iran, was brought to Europe in the 16th century where in time it became a popular spring ornamental often grown in gardens. Found in the subalpine meadows of the western Himalayas are several related species of *Fritillaria* with yellow-green, purple-spotted flowers up to 6 cm in diameter. The stems measure up to 50 cm. Fritillaries are found on south-facing grassy slopes, for instance in Cashmir, where they grow at elevations of 2,500 to 3,000 metres. Many other species of *Fritillaria* are found in eastern Siberia almost at the Arctic Circle.

Snake's Head Fritillary, Guinea Flower (306) is a moisture loving plant, found in damp mead-
Fritillaria meleagris L. ows and open riverine woods by unregulated rivers that often overflow their banks in spring. It has an underground bulb composed of two fleshy scales from which rises a loosely leaved stem drooping at the

304

top and terminated by a single bell-like flower (or two to three flowers) with closed segments and typical chequered markings. This species is distributed from the British Isles through central and southern Europe to the Caucasus and is especially characteristic of Europe's Mediterranean region.

Pheasant's-eye Daffodil (307) has several linear leaves at the base of the flattened flower stalk. *Narcissus poeticus* L. The flowers are solitary with perianth segments forming a long tube, terminated by spreading lobes with a narrow collar inside. This species is found on grassy mountain slopes in the Alps, eastern and southern Carpathians and is widely grown in its many cultivated forms in gardens throughout Europe.

Cryptanthus zonatus (Vis.) Beer (308, 309) is characterized by a low, flat leaf rosette. The leaves are up to 30 cm long, 5 cm wide, long-pointed and wavy-spiny on the margin; the upper side is patterned with irregular horizontal stripes. The flowers, arranged in a compound spike, have petals up to

6 cm long. This is a terrestrial species that grows on the ground in the deciduous tropical forests of eastern Brazil. Illustration no. 308 shows the variety *fuscus* which differs from the variety *zonatus* shown in illustration no. 309 by the colouration of the leaves.

Flamingo Plant (310) has longish lanceolate leaves with prominent stalks about 10 cm long and
Anthurium
scherzerianum
Schott
blades nearly 30 cm long. Its most attractive feature is the long-stalked inflorescence composed of a spirally curved spadix of tiny flowers subtended by a broad spathe whose striking colouration serves to attract insect pollinators. This species is native to the virgin forests of tropical America, the home of some 200 species of *Anthurium*. Well known are the many ornamental hybrids noted for the size and diverse colours of the spathes.

St. Bernard's Lily (311) has a simple erect stem terminated by a racemose inflorescence. The
Anthericum liliago L.
leaves are narrow to linear. The flowers, growing from the axils of bracts, are up to 4 cm across and coloured milky white. The perianth

307

308

309

310

segments are all the same length, three-veined, blunt and flared in full bloom. The fruit is a trilocular, many-seeded capsule. St. Bernard's Lily is found chiefly on stony, semi-steppe slopes and in open oak stands and shrubby hedgerows; wherever it grows it generally occurs in great numbers. In Europe it extends from the Iberian Peninsula throughout western, northern and southern Europe. The eastern boundary of its range extends from Denmark through western Poland and Bohemia to the western part of the Balkan Peninsula. In the wild it sometimes interbreeds with the related Spiderwort *(A. ramosum)*. These plants are dominant features of the early summer vegetation in their respective localities.

Yellow Star-of-Bethlehem (312) has a single stem growing from a single bulb and reaching *Gagea lutea* (L.) a height of 30 cm. A characteristic feature is the solitary, broadly linear, Ker-Gawl. pointed basal leaf. The stem leaves, mostly two, are keeled, lanceolate and located immediately beneath the scanty inflorescence. The flowers have long glabrous stalks growing from the axils of bracts. The perianth segments are elliptic with bluntly rounded tips, yellow within and green outside. This species is chiefly found in drier meadows, but may also be encountered in damp leafy soil in woodlands, often beside streams, mostly in lowland and hilly country. In Europe it has a practically continuous distribution from the Pyrenees to the southern Urals, its range extending to the Mediterranean region, the British Isles and in the north, in Norway, to the Arctic Circle. In Asia it occurs sporadically in Cashmir and continuously in northeastern China, Japan and Kamchatka. It has a relatively short growing period in spring so that it disappears from view in the lush herbaceous vegetation that grows later.

Meadow Yellow Star-of-Bethlehem (313) unlike the preceding species has a single, upright *Gagea pratensis* (Pers.) Dum. stem and three to five bulbs instead of one. It, too, has a solitary basal leaf, though not as wide, that is keeled and ciliate on the margin. The stem leaves are generally found beneath the inflorescence, usually three (the lowest sheath-like at the base) and have bulbils growing from the axils. The corymbose inflorescence is composed of several long-stalked flowers with shining, yellow, flared perianth segments with green stripes outside. This plant is found in rather dry grassy places, meadows and as a field weed in loamy-sandy soil from lowland to foothill districts. It is distributed in Europe from southern Sweden throughout central and southeastern Europe to Bulgaria, also locally in

311

292

312

313

Yugoslavia, Italy and France. Like other species of Yellow Star-of-Bethlehem it, too, is striking in the wild for it is always conspicuous amidst the sparse spring vegetation; its growth period, however, is very brief.

314

315

Meadow Gladiole (314) has an underground corm, erect stems with sword-shaped leaves and
Gladiolus imbricatus L. flowers arranged in a one-sided raceme. It is found chiefly in damp
meadows from central Europe east through the Ukraine to the central
Urals.

Tillandsia cyanea Linden (315) forms a dense rosette of channelled leaves up to 35 cm long, 2
cm wide and tapering to a long point. The flowers are usually arranged
in two opposite rows in a thick, simple, flat sword-like spike. The trum-
pet-like corollas of the flowers grow from the axils of striking bracts;
the stamens and stigma are concealed deep within the corolla tube.
This species grows as an epiphyte in the tropical rain forests of Ecuador.

316

Tillandsia tricholepis Baker (316) is an epiphytic species of the tropical rain forests of Brazil, Bolivia, Paraguay and Argentina. The leaves are small, about 1 cm long, 2 mm wide and circular in cross section; they are arranged on the long stem in a spiral. The flowers are arranged in a simple spike up to 5 cm long.

Meadow Saffron (317) grows from a corm buried deep in the ground. The flowers are produced *Colchicum* in autumn. They consist of a funnel-shaped perianth with segments *autumnale* L. united below into a long tube, the greater part of which is concealed underground. The individual segments are longish-ovate, pale violet and finely pubescent within. In the following spring the corm bears a stem with fleshy basal leaves enclosing a longish, trilocular capsule with a great many black-brown seeds. Sometimes the plant bears flowers in spring in which case they are greenish with large narrow perianth segments. This species is found chiefly in submontane meadows and has a relatively large area of distribution — in Europe from the British Isles to the Balkan Peninsula.

317

Slender Hyacinth (318) is a thermophilous and xerophilous species and thus found mostly in semisteppe, climatically congenial regions. It grows in open oak woods, often in sandy soil where the herb layer is not very lush. It has erect, narrowly linear leaves and stem terminated by a large number of flowers; the bottom flowers are tubular and fertile whereas those at the top are sterile and form a crest. The whole inflorescence is striking, visible in the surrounding vegetation from afar and clearly differentiated into top and bottom sections. This plant is distributed from central Europe southeastward to the eastern Mediterranean region and through Asia

Muscari tenuiflorum
Tausch

318

319

Minor to Transcaucasia; it grows scattered also in the central Ukraine, Crimea and even northern Iran. Throughout this vast range it occurs as several subspecies differing in the size of the fertile as well as sterile flowers. Some species of *Muscari* have become popular as garden ornamentals grown in masses (unlike their occurrence in the wild) to increase the impact of their blue colouring and make the effect more striking.

Grape Hyacinth (319)
Muscari racemosum
(L.) Lam. et DC.

is a robust herb with narrowly linear basal leaves that dry up from the top downward while the plant is still in flower. The flowering stem is erect and terminated by a very dense raceme of flask-like flowers coloured blue, very occasionally white. The flask-like perianth, narrowed

320

both at the base and mouth, is grooved at the top and edged with two-lobed, whitish teeth. The uppermost sterile flowers are a paler colour with white recurved teeth and nearly sessile; they do not form a crest at the top. In the wild this plant is found on sunny, grassy slopes as well as in stony fallow land, on embankments and in vineyards. Like the many related species it is distributed in central and southern Europe, extending from the Mediterranean region to northern Africa and Asia Minor. Throughout its moderately large range it is marked by great variability, particularly in the number of flowers in the inflorescence.

Neoregelia carolinae (Mez) L.B. Smith (320) is an epiphytic species of the tropical rain forests of Brazil. It forms a flat, funnel-shaped rosette of strap-shaped leaves up to 50 cm long, with pointed tips and very spiny margins. The racemose inflorescence, located in the heart of the rosette, is sessile and sheltered by the leaves in the centre, which change colour during the flowering period, remaining thus long after the flowers have faded. The petals are up to 2 cm long and spreading. The fruit is a fleshy berry.

Neoregelia concentrica L.B. Smith (321) is native to the tropical rain forests of Brazil, where it forms a leaf rosette up to 90 cm in diameter. The leaves are bluntly tipped and up to 10 cm wide. Those in the centre of the rosette change colour during the flowering period.

321

Chapter 11   PLANTS IN THE SERVICE OF MAN

It is a well known fact that plant foods form the mainstay of the diet of the world population, chiefly the peoples of Asia and South America. Plants have been of interest to man — primarily their fleshy fruits, starchy roots, tubers and seeds — from his earliest beginnings. All these formed at least part of his basic diet. Many plants also benefited him indirectly, for example as fodder for cattle, as building material, etc. It is interesting to note that in the case of many plants man first discovered those properties that made life more pleasant by taking his mind off his daily cares. Take hemp, for example. It was its intoxicating and narcotic effects that man discovered first (hashish made from the flowers and leaves) and only later its other uses — the oil from its fruits and the tough fibres from the stems, used to make rope, sailcloth, etc.

Modern man then learned to further develop the useful properties of plants to meet his needs after discovering the laws of heredity and thereby solving the mystery of the complex chemical and physical processes continuously going on in living organisms. The plant element of the biosphere became an inseparable and vital part of man's economic existence just as it had always been a vital part of his biological life.

This chapter presents plants with various useful properties but makes no attempt to determine the order of their importance to man. Be it tea plant, banana plant or flax, all are of economic importance to man, who has taken full advantage of their useful properties and has come to regard them solely as plants serving his needs. In many instances, however, we are not fully acquainted with or else not fully convinced of the useful properties of the plants. For example we are well acquainted with the therapeutic effects of many herbs. The tradition of folk medicine and herb healers is a very old one but we often forget that medicinal herbs have specific effects and if misused may be detrimental rather than beneficial to the human organism. For that reason many should not be used without first consulting a physician. Despite this, medicinal herbs rank high on the list of plants useful to man.

323

This chapter does not deal only with plants of economic importance, however. A plant's usefulness to man may be perceived in a broader context. Plants that are simply attractive, fragrant and colourful are also important. Their beauty is pleasing to the eye and makes man more perceptive of his environment and more appreciative of nature. Plants are increasingly becoming man's constant companions not only in parks and gardens but also in the home. Man is learning to know them, improve them by breeding and selection, and first and foremost to protect them.

Hibiscus schizopetalus Hook. fil. (322) text see page 308

Tea Plant (323) is known to all mankind for it is the leaves of this plant that are used to make
Camellia sinensis (L.) O. Kuntze — the popular beverage — tea. It is a shrub with short-stalked, finely toothed leaves and flowers growing singly in the leaf axils. The fruit is a capsule with large globose seeds. The genus *Camellia* embraces approximately 45 species native to the mountain forests of southeastern Asia but grown on plantations in the subtropical regions of all monsoon Asia and also locally in the temperate regions of the northern hemisphere (Transcaucasia) where climatic conditions are suitable for the purpose. The flowers of some members of this genus are sometimes used to perfume Chinese tea.

Wild Strawberry (324) is a Eurasian species with a widespread distribution extending from
Fragaria vesca L. — Iceland to eastern Siberia. It is a member of the genus which includes the popular cultivated species grown for their sweet 'berries' (the real

fruit is not the 'berry' itself, the fleshy receptacle, but the small achenes covering its surface). The Wild Strawberry is common in sunny woodland clearings and on shrubby slopes and is likewise often found in screes and on alluvial deposits. The flowers, arranged in a terminal umbel, have white petals covered with appressed hairs and spreading sepals. The berry is longish-ovoid and up to 2 cm long. The leaves of this plant contain tannins and essential oils and were formerly brewed to make a tea used in folk medicine. However attention was focussed chiefly on the fruits and their delicious flavour resulting in the intensive breeding of the North American species.

Strawberry (325), native to North America, is widely grown throughout Europe for its tasty, *Fragaria virginiana* Duch. irregular, globose, deep red accessory fruits or 'berries'. More widely cultivated is the hybrid between this and the South American *F. chiloënsis* Duch., designated as *F. × ananassa* Duch. *(F. virginiana × F. chiloënsis)*. The stem and leaves are covered with short appressed hairs and the sepals are pressed loosely to the berry. As the large berries ripen the stems are bent to the ground by their weight.

Hibiscus rosa-sinensis L. cv. Cooperi (326), cv. Floridus (327), cv. Luteus (328) is a beautiful shrub occurring in many varieties in the tropical regions of the Old and New World where it flowers throughout the year. In some countries (for example in some Indian states) Hibiscus is the national flower, one

325

326

327

306

whose extraordinary beauty has won it wide-spread popularity and esteem. It belongs to the bombax (Bombaceae) family, which includes many well known, economically important plants such as cotton. The blossoms are large with a calyx that is often cup-shaped and either undivided or shallowly lobed and colourful petals that are usually downy outside. The numerous stamens are joined to form a long tube that protrudes from the flower. The ovary develops into a capsule with many seeds.

The genus *Hibiscus* embraces some 200 species, the most variable being the one illustrated here which is cultivated in a great many forms differing widely in the size and colour of the flowers. It is native to eastern India and China where it reaches a height of 5 metres, which makes it a small tree. The leaves are glossy, prominently veined, pointed-ovate in outline and crenate on the margin, sometimes entire at the base. An outstanding feature of this species is that it flowers from spring until autumn. The petals come in a wide range of delicate hues with darker margins made more striking by being wavy. The whole effect is underscored by the central tube of stamens.

There is no denying that Hibiscus beautifies the places where it grows, be it in the wild, in the greenhouse or in the home. Many related tropical species are of economic importance, for instance the Asian species *H. cannabinus* is important for its fibre, so called Bombay hemp, and most contain important glycosides (complex organic substances) used in medicine.

328

Hibiscus schizopetalus Hook. fil. (322), native to tropical eastern Africa, is noted for its extraordinary long-stalked flowers. The calyx is tubular and the corollas deeply laciniate with recurved lobes thereby accentuating all the more the effect of the long, curving tube, terminated by numerous 4-locular anthers and the style.

Dyer's Greenweed (329) brightens shrubby slopes and dry open broad-leaved woods with its
Genista tinctoria L.   presence. It is also found in hedgerows and pasturelands from lowland to foothill districts throughout practically all of Europe and all western and central Siberia, Asia Minor and the Caucasus. Throughout this vast range it is naturally extremely variable and occurs as several subspecies differing in the flowers and fruits. It contains large amounts of essential oils and tannins and for this reason was used in folk medicine as a disinfectant and diuretic. As the scientific name *tinctoria* indicates it was formerly used as a dye for it contains the yellow colouring

329

330

matter genistein. The much branched stems are grooved and without spines but covered at the top with appressed hairs. The leaves are alternate, dark green above, paler green and ciliate beneath with prominent lateral veins. The golden-yellow flowers are arranged in terminal, many-flowered racemes.

Lupin (330) is a North American plant that rapidly became naturalized elsewhere. It became
Lupinus perennis L. popular not only as an ornamental in parks and gardens but chiefly as food for bees and forest animals. Its large, often spreading masses brighten woodland clearings and forest margins in summer. In Europe it is also grown as a field crop used for green manure. The stem is nearly one metre high, softly hairy, practically unbranched and terminated by a dense inflorescence that increases conspicuously in length during the flowering period. The leaves are stalked and palmately divided into seven to ten leaflets that are longish-ovate in outline with soft points, glabrous on the upper surface and covered with random hairs beneath. The flowers open in succession from the bottom of the raceme upward. They are large with a bilabiate calyx and a corolla coloured blue, sometimes tinged violet, very occasionally white or pink. Diversity of colour is a typical characteristic of all members of the genus.

331

Lesser Periwinkle (331) is procumbent, semi-shrubby perennial with shining, short-stalked
Vinca minor L. leaves coloured a paler green on the underside and faintly revolute
margins. The flowers are solitary and grow on long stalks from the leaf
axils. Lesser Periwinkle is found in open woods, woodland margins,
copses and often also on stony ground covered with thickets. It contains a number of alkaloids and is thus an important source of medicinal substances with a wide range of uses not fully known as yet. It is
also a decorative plant grown for its attractive shining foliage and
equally attractive flowers. Breeding and selection have produced countless varieties differing markedly in the colour of the flowers (for instance cv. Cuprea, cv. Azurea, cv. Alba, cv. Rosea, etc.). The genus
Vinca includes approximately ten species, mostly native to Europe —
only three are found in the tropics. Besides various alkaloids they also
contain caoutchouc-like substances.

Austrian Flax (332) is a thermophilous species found on limestone slopes. The flowers, ar-
Linum austriacum L. ranged in dense, one-sided racemes, are stalked and have dark-veined
petals. The plant is tufted and thickly covered with linear leaves. This
species is related to the ancient flax of commerce *(L. usitatissimum)*
whose seeds are used to make linseed oil and whose stem fibres are
spun into linen thread. The genus *Linum* embraces approximately 200
species distributed in the subtropical and temperate regions of the
earth.

310

Lathyrus pannonicus (Jacq.) Garcke (333) is a beautiful albeit inconspicuous plant of steppe, mainly limestone slopes. Many species of the genus *Lathyrus* are widely grown for their pretty fragrant flowers and are a decorative element in the garden as well as in the wild. The large flowers in scanty, one-sided, stalked racemes always add a bright note to the spring and summer vegetation.

Earth-nut Pea (334) is
Lathyrus tuberosus L.
widespread throughout the Mediterranean and temperate regions of Europe with a continuous distribution from northern Spain to the Urals, including the entire Black Sea region. In Asia it is found in Transcaucasia, in Kazakhstan and as far as central Siberia. The northern boundary of its range in Europe extends approximately from Belgium through northern Germany and Poland eastward through the

332

333

311

Ukraine and central Volga region to the Urals; it was introduced to Great Britain. It is a species with flowers that are not only pretty but also delicately scented, their fragrance almost on a par with that of the cultivated southern European Sweet Pea *(L. odoratus)*. It has a scrambling stem that is sharply four-angled but not winged and the leaflets are patterned with network veining. The one-sided racemes are composed of drooping flowers up to 1.5 cm long, coloured carmine-red, dark violet or whitish. This uncommonly varied species grows in fallow land and as a weed in fields. It often occurs on unfirm ground by roadside ditches and on railway embankments. If it grows close to shrubs or even trees it rapidly catches hold of these vertical supports and climbs upward.

334

335

Sainfoin (335) is a
*Onobrychis
viciaefolia* Scop.
Eurasian plant with many related species in the eastern Mediterranean region and Asia Minor. Its area of distribution indicates that it is definitely a thermophilous plant, one marked by variability and found on sunny grassy and stony slopes. The variety *sativa,* more robust with pale carmine-red flowers, is cultivated as a forage crop. In the wild it is a perennial with shortly branched, furrowed, angled stems covered with appressed hairs. The leaves are divided into linear leaflets that are silky-hairy on the underside. The flowers, up to 1 cm long, are in dense, long-stalked racemes that are cylindrical in shape before the flowers open. The calyx is bell-shaped with shortly ciliate teeth, the corolla is pinkish-red, occasionally white with the largest petal veined dark red. The pods are flat and tubercled on the lower margin.

Thorn-apple (336) is a
Datura suaveolens
H.B.K.
native of Mexico. It has alternate, stalked, entire leaves and large flowers, up to 30 cm long, with a tubular calyx and a long, trumpet-shaped corolla with five large, regular lobes. Some South American and eastern African species of *Datura* yield important drugs for the pharmaceutical industry. They contain alkaloids (principally hyoscyamine) used to treat asthma. Crossing of some of these species has produced hybrids with large concentrations of these effective substances.

313

Coral Tree (337) is an extraordinarily attractive plant containing complex erythrine alkaloids
Erythrina crista-galli L. used for pharmaceutical purposes. It is a twining subshrub of the
Brazilian tropics with longish-elliptical, pointed, pale green leaves, usually trifoliolate, and beautiful flowers, up to 5 cm long, resembling a cockerel's head in shape and even colour. Grown in greenhouses are several varieties differing in the size of the leaves and colour of the flowers.

Common Elder (338) is a shrub or small tree commonly found in broad-leaved woods, shoreline
Sambucus nigra L. thickets, floodplain forests as well as on stony ground and in waste places. It is distributed chiefly in the southern and temperate regions of

336

337

Europe, extending to the Middle East. The branches as well as the annual shoots have a thick white pith. The leaves are composed of elliptical leaflets with serrate margins. The yellowish flowers are arranged in flat terminal inflorescences and have a strong fragrance, interesting with the first whiff but rather unpleasant later. The fruits, clustered in drooping heads, are shining, blackish violet, globose berries containing three seeds. The Common Elder is noted for its medicinal properties, the parts collected for this purpose being the flowers, which contain large concentrations of essential oils, and the fruits, which contain tannins, organic acids and vitamins. All these substances are used in treating diseases of the respiratory passages and painful neuralgias.

Hazel (339). is distributed throughout all Europe to the Urals, including Asia Minor and the
Corylus avellana L. Caucasus. It is an important tree of open broad-leaved woods and from time immemorial has been cultivated for its oily nuts and in certain forms as an ornamental. The leaves, which contain essential oils and

315

338

tannins, were also formerly used in herbal tea mixtures for their diuretic effects but are now used mostly in the cosmetic industry.

Common or British Oak (340) is a large, broad-leaved tree reaching a height of 40 metres. It is
Quercus robur L.   so striking that its image figures prominently in every broad-leaved forest and it is the principal tree in oak woods on moist, leafy soils as well as on sandy substrates from lowland to hilly country. Its range is extensive but confined mostly to Europe, extending from the British Isles, southern Norway and Sweden in the north and Spain, Sicily and Greece in the south continuously to western Siberia. The young twigs are angled and hairy and the bark, particularly that of old trees, is deeply furrowed. The leaves, markedly varied in shape, are short-stalked, bluntly lobed, hairy at first, later glabrous, and leathery. They are shed in autumn. The male flowers are in drooping catkins, the female flowers in scanty clusters at the tips of the branches. The fruits are acorns, enclosed at the base by a softly hairy cupule. This oak is highly prized for its wood and the bark contains high concentrations of tannins and acids which have an anti-inflammatory action. The acorns, too, are important, as food for woodland creatures, and last but not least the tree itself is a decorative element of parks, particularly as a solitary specimen.

339

340

Castor-oil Plant (341) is a native of tropical Africa, and perhaps also India and Pakistan, where
Ricinus communis L. it is a tree. In temperate regions, for instance in Europe, it is grown as an annual. Its cathartic effects have been known and used since days of old. It is prized chiefly for its seeds, which contain proteins and alkaloids in addition to castor oil that does not oxidize on exposure to air; the latter is an important raw material in the cosmetic industry. The oil is poisonous but is rendered non-toxic by boiling with water. The plant has a stout, glabrous, pruinose, slightly branched stem covered with large, alternate, long-stalked, palmately divided leaves. The flowers are arranged in dense terminal racemes with male flowers at the bottom and female flowers at the top, and are softly spiny. The stamens are very attractive with numerous anthers and filaments arranged like an umbrella. The female flowers have long, forked stigmas coloured red. The fruit, a trilocular, spiny capsule, splits into three sections at maturity; the seeds are oval with marbled markings.

341

342

Banana (342) is a plant that needs no introduction for everyone is acquainted with its tasty, *Musa sapientum* L. edible fruit. Like many other plants noted for their fruit it is grown in many varieties in the tropical regions of the Old and New World. These are robust herbaceous plants of tree-like habit with leaves arranged in a spiral and forming what appears to be a trunk. Rising from this column of leaf sheaths is a stem with a racemose inflorescence. The flowers have a tubular calyx, inconspicuous corolla and five stamens.

319

Common St. John's Wort (343) is a herb that figures prominently in folklore for its miraculous
Hypericum effects. However it is important not only in folk medicine but also in
perforatum L. the modern pharmaceutical industry. Glands on the leaves contain
a bitter oil and release a red colouring matter when rubbed between
the fingers. The green top parts are highly prized as a drug for the
essential oils, pigments and tannins they contain. This species is distributed throughout all Europe, Asia and northern Africa. It is found chiefly
on sunny grassy slopes, in dry meadows and in pastures as well as in
scrub and in open woodlands. It is a robust perennial with erect,
rounded stems, glandular beneath the inflorescence and branched at
the top. The leaves are elliptical, entire, glabrous and covered with
translucent glandular dots. The fragrant flowers, arranged in a broad,
terminal raceme, have black-glandular stalks, a pointed calyx dotted
with black, and golden-yellow corolla likewise dotted black. The fruit is
a glandular-dotted capsule. *H. perforatum* has many related species
which, apart from a few exceptions, are found in dry, open places on
slopes and in woodlands. It may be said that all are decorative elements of the plant community.

Centaury (344) is distributed from the Azores throughout Europe and through the Ukraine and
Centaurium Caucasus to Iran, extending in northern Europe to southern Sweden
umbellatum Gilib. and Finland. It often occurs in masses in woodland clearings, open
scrub and on sunny slopes. A characteristic feature are the terminal

343

344

345

dichasial cymes of shapely flowers coloured pinkish-red, very occasionally white. The bitter substances, concentrated chiefly in the flowers and flowering stems, were a popular drug in folk medicine used in the form of a bitter tea to promote digestion.

Pineapple (345, 346), a native of central Venezuela, is nowadays grown in tropical regions *Ananas comosus* throughout the world for its tasty edible collective fruit, which has (L.) Merrill a sweet fragrance and golden-yellow flesh and is eaten raw or cooked in syrup after removing the hard rind and woody core. The fruit is topped by a crest of green leaves which serve as a means of asexual reproduction. Besides the pineapples grown on plantations for their fruit there are also ornamental varieties such as the illustrated cv. Variegatus which has leaves edged pale yellow and is an unusual and attractive specimen for room decoration.

346

347

348

Momordica charantia L. (347) is an annual with a prostrate stem up to 2 metres long. The fruits ripen in the autumn. The genus *Momordica* includes approximately 65 species found in the tropics of Africa and Asia where the edible fruits are often preserved in salt and are an important ingredient of piquant sauces.

Cucumber (348) is probably native to eastern India and has several related species native to southwestern Asia and eastern Africa. It is a trailing, occasionally climbing, annual vine with leaves that are alternate, undivided and shallowly palmately lobed. The flowers, growing singly from the axils of the leaves, are golden-yellow and have a bell-shaped calyx and a five-lobed, bell-funnel-shaped corolla. Characteristic features of the species are the pointed lobes of the leaves and the long cylindrical fruit, which varies in shape, colour and surface texture in the many cultivated varieties. The genus *Cucumis* includes approximately 25 species distributed primarily in the subtropical and tropical regions of Africa and Asia.

Cucumis sativus L.

323

Coffee (351), native to eastern Africa, is one of the most economically important species of the
Coffea arabica L.   genus which includes approximately 60 native to tropical Africa and Madagascar. Coffee is grown in numerous hybrid forms in tropical South America (Brazil, Colombia, etc.). It is an evergreen shrub with fragrant flowers in dense axillary clusters. A characteristic feature of Coffee is that it produces flowers the whole year long so that one may find flowers and fruits in all the various stages of development on a single plant. The fruit, a two-seeded drupe, is green at first, later becoming yellow, then red and finally violet-black. The bean-like seeds, for which the plant is cultivated, contain caffein. After the pericarp is removed they are roasted, ground and brewed to make the familiar beverage.

Zig-zag Clover (352) belongs to the genus *Trifolium* which includes first and foremost forage
Trifolium medium L.   and nectar-producing plants. The illustrated species is not noted for its economic importance but is without doubt an attractive plant of open broad-leaved woods and grassy slopes as well as pasturelands and meadows. Its branched stems are covered with appressed hairs and the leaves are divided into finely toothed leaflets that are hairy on the underside and glabrous with a reddish-brown band above. The flowers are in globose to ovoid heads. This species is distributed throughout all Europe, extending in the east through the Urals to western Siberia.

352

Spiny Rest-harrow (353), also distributed throughout Europe, is a low, spiny subshrub and is
Ononis spinosa L. found mostly in dry grassy places — meadows, pastures, hedgerows, slopes — chiefly on volcanic rock substrates including limestones. It is first and foremost a medicinal herb (the root contains saponins and a small amount of essential oils), which together with certain other umbelliferous plants has a diuretic effect. The drug is used in herbal tea mixtures in the treatment of kidney diseases. The stems, which become woody, are much branched, thorny and covered with large, glandular-hairy leaves that soon fall. The flowers occur on short branches in loose racemes, are up to 2 cm long and coloured deep pink to white. They are produced practically the whole summer long.

Broad Bean (354) is native to Europe's Mediterranean region and northern Africa and has been
Vicia faba L. grown throughout Europe for fodder since time immemorial. It is an annual herb with erect, usually unbranched, sharply four-angled stems

353

354

about 50 cm high. The leaves are fleshy, pale green, and divided into sessile, ovate leaflets with entire margin. In fields where it is grown in large masses its large colourful flowers make an attractive display. They are faintly scented, short-stalked and arranged in axillary clusters. The calyx is tubular and turns black at the base, the corolla is white and the upper largest petal (standard) is patterned with violet or brown veins. The lateral petals (wings) have a large blackish-violet blotch. The pods are dark brown when ripe and often hairy; the beans themselves are a popular domestic vegetable and are harvested when the pods are still green and fleshy.

356 357

Gorse or Furze (355), native to western Europe, is a shrub up to 2 metres high with dark green
Ulex europaeus L. branches and short spiny twigs. The leaves are usually spiny or scale-like; the flowers are in twos or threes on the short twigs, often growing on stalks up to 1 cm long from the axils of the spines. The genus *Ulex* includes approximately 25 species distributed primarily in western Europe and northern Africa. To the central European they are reminiscent of the broom *(Sarothamnus)* common in those areas. Gorse is planted out as a solitary specimen on grassy slopes and near the sea-coast to bind sandy-loamy soils and prevent erosion by the wind.

Wood Goatsbeard (356) has an extensive but very interrupted range of distribution in the
Aruncus dioicus northern hemisphere. In Europe it is distributed from the Rhine region
(Walt.) Fern. (syn. eastward to the Black Sea region and the Caucasus; central Italy and
Aruncus sylvestris the Pyrenees mark its southernmost boundary and central Poland its
Kostel.) northern limit. In Asia it is found only in the Far East from Kamchatka through Japan to southern China with a sporadic occurrence in Kashmir. In North America it is encountered on the Pacific coast and from the midwest to the Atlantic coast. Wood Goatsbeard reaches a height of 2 metres and has dense terminal inflorescences composed of a great many small unisexual flowers. The male flowers are yellowish-white,

331

the female flowers pure white. It grows in shaded damp woods, ravine thickets and woodland clearings, mainly in foothill and mountain districts.

Wild Cabbage (357) is
Brassica oleracea
L. var. *acephala*
DC.

grown for decoration, as are other ornamental varieties such as var. *laciniata* and var. *palmifolia.* It is a biennial with a stem that becomes woody at the base, branches at the top and is bluish pruinose in colour. The leaves are stalked and lyrate, the upper stem leaves are lobed with revolute margins. The flowers are in terminal racemes. The fruits, cylindrical and sometimes up to 10 cm long, are stalked and spreading. Better known than these ornamental forms are the edible varieties of *B. oleracea* such as cauliflower, kohlrabi, cabbage and Savoy.

Sisal (358) has a simple
Agave sisalana
Perrine

stem up to 1 metre high growing from a dense rosette of thick fleshy leaves nearly 1.5 metre long. This species, like all the approximately 300 members of the genus, does not flower for many years; not until the end of its life span does it bear huge spikes up to 6 metres long composed of green flowers about 5 cm long. These are produced once and after the fruits mature the plant dies. The strong fibres obtained from the leaves of this species are used for making rope, sacking, insulation, etc. and the plant, native to Mexico like most other agaves, is grown for this purpose on large plantations in Central America.

358

359

360

Coconut Palm (359) has a tall, slender trunk terminated by a bunch of large stalked leaves. The
Cocos nucifera L. leaf blades are entire at first, later divided into huge fans several metres in length. The flowers are arranged in a dense spadix enclosed by a spathe and grow from the axils of the leaf-stalks. Most important are the fruits (coconuts) which are used in many ways. The oil obtained from the dried meat is used as a food and for making soap, the meat is shredded for use in confectionery, and the prepared fibre of the husks (coir) is used in manufacturing matting, bagging, sails, ropes, etc. The Coconut Palm is probably indigenous to Polynesia, where it grows beside the coast, but is grown in most tropical regions throughout the world.

Papaya (360) is native to the West Indies (the Caribbean region) and is now grown in all
Carica papaja L. tropical regions of the world for its tasty fruit. The trunk, which reaches a height of 3 to 10 metres, is terminated by a whorl of stalked leaves with clusters (racemes) of flowers growing from the axils. From the female flowers develop large, oblong fruits up to 30 cm long and reminiscent of melons in shape, consistency, flavour and fra-

333

grance; they are yellow or orange and contain a great many black seeds. In the tropics this species is often grown in seedless form and the white 'milk' obtained from the unripe fruits is used in medicine for the alkaloids contained therein.

Common Mallow (361) is distributed from Scandinavia to northern Africa and sporadically in
Malva sylvestris L.   Asia; in North America and the southern hemisphere it is an introduced species. It is used in folk medicine for the mucilaginous substances and tannins it contains, which have an anti-inflammatory effect (subsp. *mauritiana* is more important in this respect than the one shown in the illustration). The petals are a lovely colour with three dark veins.

361

362

Common Horse Chestnut (362) is a handsome tree often planted out in tree avenues and as an
ornamental in parks. It forms spreading stands in the southwestern part
of the Balkan Peninsula (in the Yugoslavian republic of Macedonia), in
northern Greece and in part of Albania; elsewhere it is a cultivated
tree. The high concentration of saponins in the seeds made this a popular drug used in the treatment of catarrh of the upper respiratory passages. The leaves have very long stalks and are palmate with irregularly toothed margins and reddish-brown hairs covering the entire underside at first; later they are pubescent only along the veins. The flowers
are in erect, conical racemes. The fruit is a very striking, spiny capsule
containing glossy brown seeds ('conkers') used to feed wild animals in
game preserves. Shown in the illustration is the pink flowered hybrid
A. × carnea obtained by crossing *A. hippocastanum* with other species.

*Aesculus
hippocastanum* L.

Tomato (363) is a South American plant that gained widespread popularity as soon as man discovered its tasty, vitamin-rich, edible berries. These may vary in shape and colour — besides red they may be yellow or even white. The plant is an annual sometimes reaching a height of 50 cm, glandular-pubescent to hairy along its entire length and with a pronounced aroma that may even be slightly unpleasant. The stems are branched, the leaves pinnate with leaflets that are stalked, pointed and finely pubescent. The flowers, arranged in relatively dense lateral cymes, have hairy, linear-lanceolate sepals and a yellow rotate or bell-shaped corolla deeply divided into long pointed lobes. Besides Vitamin C the fruit also contains tannins. The Tomato is sometimes classed in the genus *Solanum,* which includes other economically important plants (for instance potato and eggplant) as well as many decorative species, primarily from Mexico, South America, India and Sri Lanka.

Lycopersicon lycopersicum (L.) Karst. ex Fatw.

363

364

Common Laburnum (364), native to southern Europe, bears a profusion of magnificent yellow
Laburnum flowers in loose pendulous racemes. It is primarily grown for decora-
anagyroides Med. tion in parks and gardens though formerly use was also made of the
drug from the seeds. These contain alkaloids with effects much like
those of nicotine and were used with the leaves as a substitute for
tobacco.

Passion Flower (365) is a Brazilian species flowering from summer until autumn. The lower
Passiflora racemosa leaves are orbicular, the upper leaves three-lobed. The flowers, up to
Brot. 12 cm in diameter, have recurved petals thereby making the white-
based corona and the ring of stamens all the more striking. *P. racemosa*
is one of the most rewarding species for growing in small heated glass-
houses. The genus includes approximately 250 species distributed in
the tropical regions of America, Asia and Australia.

337

365

366

Passion Flower (366) is a beautiful species from tropical America where it is called Grenadilla

Passiflora
quadrangularis L.

by the natives for its berries are very tasty. It is a climbing shrub with smooth winged stems and short-stalked, rounded-ovate leaves. These have entire margins, pointed tips and heart-shaped bases. The flowers, with ovoid petals, are amongst the largest sported by the members of this genus — they measure up to 12 cm across. The corona filaments, arranged in five rows, are curly and coloured white at the base and tip and carmine in the centre. The berries are yellow-green and up to 22 cm long. The variety *variegata* with yellow-spotted leaves is grown in greenhouses.

Passion Flower (367) is a Brazilian species with shapely, regular flowers which also has edible

Passiflora edulis
Sims.

berries that are esteemed as dessert fruit — grenadillas. The scientific as well as the vernacular name for these flowers is based on the supposed resemblance of their various parts to the instruments of Christ's suffering. The calyx and corolla form a fleshy structure edged with a fringed corona and with a peculiar three-branched structure between the pistil and ring of stamens.

338

Red Currant (368), from western Europe, is a dense shrub up to 2 metres high, widely grown for
Ribes rubrum L.   its tasty, slightly sour, red, yellowish or white berries. It has become an
important plant of commerce cultivated on a large scale. Vitamin C is
found in the berries of all currants but is present in the greatest concentrations in those of the Black Currant *(R. nigrum)*, which also contain
tannins and acids. The leaves of Black Currant are likewise important
for they contain essential oils and are added to herbal tea mixtures. The
twigs of *R. rubrum* are spineless and covered with random hairs; the
leaves are palmately lobed, irregularly toothed on the margin and pubescent on the undersurface. The flowers, clustered in racemes, are small
and greenish.

Gooseberry (369) has tasty though somewhat bland fruit and is widely grown in numerous
Ribes grossularia L.   garden varieties; it also becomes naturalized readily. The wilding species is found in open woods and on overgrown shrubby stony slopes
both in lowland and mountain districts. The fruits are ovoid to globose
berries coloured yellow-green or reddish and hairy; they are always
smaller than those of cultivated forms. *R. grossularia* is a spiny shrub
up to 1.5 metres high with crenately lobed leaves and flowers borne
singly or in clusters. The calyx is bell-shaped and hairy and is conspicuously longer than the whitish corolla.

368

369

370

373

Apple (372) is a shrub or tree up to 5 metres high. The branches are usually felted at first, later
Malus floribunda glabrous and reddish-brown with broadly ovate, deeply toothed leaves.
Sieb. The leaf blades are glossy, glabrous and hairy only along the main ribs
on the upper surface. The fruits (pomes) are globose and variously
coloured. This woody plant is native to the Amur region in the Far East
and is grown for decoration in many varieties, differing in the size and
colour of the pomes and in the shape of the leaf blade.

Rose (373) with its large red blossoms calls to mind the many noble characteristics associated
Rosa majalis J. with the large genus *Rosa* — the rose hips rich in Vitamin C and the
Herrmann em. exquisite fragrance of the attar made from the petals of certain southern
Mansf. European species. Roses are grown all over the world for these quali-
ties and for the beauty of the flowers of the many cultivated forms and
hybrids.